Designing Organizations

Designing Organizations

An Executive Guide to Strategy, Structure, and Process

—New and Revised—

Jay R. Galbraith

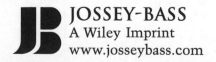
JOSSEY-BASS
A Wiley Imprint
www.josseybass.com

Published by Jossey-Bass
A Wiley Imprint
989 Market Street, San Francisco, CA 94103-1741   www.josseybass.com

Jossey-Bass books and products are available through most bookstores. To contact Jossey-Bass directly
call our Customer Care Department within the U.S. at 800-956-7739, outside the U.S. at 317-572-3986,
or fax 317-572-4002.

Jossey-Bass also publishes its books in a variety of electronic formats. Some content that appears in
print may not be available in electronic books.

Library of Congress Cataloging-in-Publication Data
Galbraith, Jay R.
   Designing organizations : an executive guide to strategy, structure,
      and process / by Jay R. Galbraith.—New and revised ed.
         p.   cm.—(The Jossey-Bass business & management series)
   Includes bibliographical references and index.
   ISBN 0-7879-5745-3 (alk. paper)
   1. Organizational effectiveness.   2. Strategic planning.   I. Title.   II. Series.
   HD58.9 .G35   2002
   658.4¢012—dc21   2001003155

Printed in the United States of America
FIRST EDITION
HB Printing   20 19 18 17 16 15 14 13 12 11

The Jossey-Bass Business & Management Series

Contents

Table, Figures, and Exhibits

Chapter 5

Chapter 6

Chapter 7

Chapter 8

Chapter 9

Chapter 10

Preface

The revised edition of *Designing Organizations* is the result of two factors coming together. First, I had accumulated some new material since the book first appeared in 1995. A lot of this material came from a project at the International Institute for Management Development (IMD) in Lausanne, Switzerland, where I was a faculty member from 1995 to 2000. The project grew out of a survey called the CEO's Agenda, conducted by my colleague, Ulrich Steger. In the survey, he discovered that CEOs were putting a high priority on "managing organizational complexity." So I followed up on the issue and scheduled interviews with the CEOs of many of the companies that were part of IMD's Partner Network. Some of the ideas that resulted from the interviews made up the content of the second half of my book *Designing the Global Corporation* (2000). I also presented the ideas at a conference at the Wharton School in March 1999. Paired with me in one of the sessions was Nathaniel Foote, who leads McKinsey's Organization Design Practice. He and some of his colleagues were pursuing a project labeled "Managing Multiple Dimensions." Their clients, too, were wrestling with the issue of organizational complexity. Nathaniel asked if I would join with them on their project.

The next phase was a project jointly sponsored by IMD and McKinsey & Company. Several of IMD's partner companies volunteered to be case study subjects. The project came to be known as "Organizing Around the Customer." The cases from the study make up some of the new examples that update the material in the revised edition. The study is also the basis for a new chapter of the same title. Some of the examples also deal with the complexities of managing and using the Internet. So I have added a new discussion of electronic coordination, especially the use of e-coordination to manage interactions with the customer. So the ideas of organizing around the customer, managing multiple dimensions, and e-coordination are the primary additions that constitute the revised edition.

A second factor was a suggestion from Diane Downey and Amy Kates of Downey Associates International to collaborate on a workbook, or tool kit, to accompany *Designing Organizations*. Many of my clients had asked me if I had any tools or materials that could help them in designing their own organizations. I always had to respond in the negative because I am poor at creating these kinds of materials. As it turned out, Diane and Amy had been taking my work and creating just the kinds of tools and materials that people were asking for, so collaboration with them seemed the natural thing to do. But it seemed to be a better idea to pair the workbook with the new material that I was generating. The result was this revision of *Designing Organizations* and the creation of *Designing Dynamic Organizations* (Galbraith, Downey, and Kates), both of which will appear in 2001.

I would like to thank Nathaniel Foote and his colleagues at McKinsey for their support of the research that led to many of the ideas in this revised edition. And as always, I would like to thank my partner, Sasha Galbraith. Her skilled management of our affairs gives me the time I need to do the writing.

Breckenridge, Colorado   Jay R. Galbraith
September 2001

About the Author

An internationally recognized expert on organization design, Jay R. Galbraith helps major global corporations create capability for competing in the new century. His work focuses on the areas of organization design, change, and development; strategy and organization at the corporate, business unit, and international levels; and international partnering arrangements including joint ventures and network-type organizations. He is currently examining organizational units that are rapidly reconfigurable to suit quickly changing demands of customers and markets across multinational boundaries. Galbraith consults regularly with clients in the United States, Europe, Asia, and South America. His most recent book, *Designing the Global Corporation,* describes how leading multinational corporations deal with demands of their increasingly global customers to provide solutions, not just products.

Galbraith is professor emeritus at the International Institute for Management Development (IMD) in Lausanne, Switzerland. He is also a senior research scientist at the Center for Effective Organizations at the University of Southern California. Prior to joining the faculty at USC, he directed his own management consulting firm. He has previously been on the faculty of the Wharton School at the University of Pennsylvania and the Sloan School of Management at MIT. He has a degree in chemical engineering and both MBA and DBA degrees from Indiana University.

Galbraith has written numerous articles for professional journals, handbooks, and research collections. His book, *Tomorrow's Organization: Crafting Winning Capabilities in a Dynamic World* (Jossey-Bass, 1998), was a cooperative project with Sue Mohrmann, Edward E. Lawler III, and the Center for Effective Organizations. It is a solution-oriented guidebook for creating organizations capable of competing in the next century. *Competing with Flexible Lateral Organizations* (Addison-Wesley, 1994) explores management through less hierarchical team structures. His award-winning *Organizing for the Future* (Jossey-Bass, 1993) is a compilation of ten years of research done by the Center for Effective Organizations.

Designing Organizations

1

Introduction

Six Immutable Forces Shaping Today's Organizations

A few years ago, top managers were not interested in organization, let alone in acquiring a superior understanding of it or skill in its creation. Organization was perceived to be something about charts and job descriptions—necessary evils or bureaucratic activities.

Then the basis of competition shifted and organizing slowly moved toward the top of management's agenda. Leaders began to recognize they needed to understand the principles and the tools that would allow them to create organizations superior to those of their competitors. One of the changes is illustrated by the graph shown in Figure 1.1.

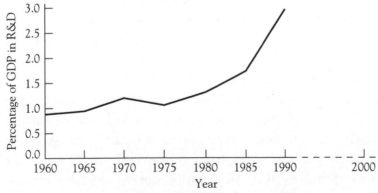

FIGURE 1.1. Percentage of GDP Invested in R&D.

Source: Dertouzes, Lester, and Solow, 1989, p. 58; "R&D Scoreboard," June 1992.

The graph shows that most countries began investing more of their gross domestic product (GDP) in research and development (R&D) every year about twenty-five years ago, and the rate of increase has continued to climb. The developed countries were moving to higher value-added products, while developing countries adopted less sophisticated, higher labor-content products to the same result.

The increased investment in R&D means that the companies in developed countries create value for customers by putting knowledge and design into their products. This "knowledge difference" can be illustrated by comparing the microprocessor with the dynamic random access memory (DRAM), both semiconductor products consisting of equal numbers of transistors on a chip. The DRAM is a blank commodity chip awaiting information. The microprocessor, in contrast, contains sophisticated circuit designs and architectures to achieve unbelievably fast computations, and it sells for ten times the price of the commodity DRAM chip.

The circuit designs on the microprocessor represent the brains and energy of the engineers who created them. It is they who create value for customers in the new economy. So the assets of Intel and Motorola are actually the knowledge and energy of the engineers who create the designs. The ability of Intel and Motorola to compete in the new economy depends on their ability to attract, retain, motivate, and coordinate talented engineers. In short, it depends on organization of the efforts of these engineers.

A second change is that companies now compete in a world of temporary advantage. The cycle time of just about everything is being drastically reduced (Hout and Bower, 1998). The new product development cycle, the product life cycle, and the order-to-delivery cycle are all being constantly reduced. Managements recognize that time is money. And the more time that is taken out of the business processes, the more money is available for other investments. Similarly, the time duration during which a competitive advantage lasts is also being reduced. Think of your own business. If you introduce a service or product that gives you an advantage, how long does it last before a competitor matches or exceeds that advantage? It takes a couple of weeks to duplicate a new derivative product in investment banking. It takes a couple of months to match the advantage of a new laser printer. The winner in the laser printer business is the company that can produce one advantage after another, each lasting about two months. The winner will be the company with the best new product development process. In short, in an era of temporary advantage, you compete with your organization.

Third, the R&D investment raises the fixed costs of doing business. For many companies in many industries domestic demand is no longer sufficient to cover their fixed costs. These companies must seek additional demand outside their home countries. When a lot of companies expand into other countries the result is heightened global competition. Today, in addition to traditional domestic rivals—those that have survived—there are Japanese and European rivals and an increasing tide of imports from emerging market countries. These new competitors often play by different rules. They also give our customers more choices. As customers learn how to benefit from the greater range of choices, suppliers need to learn how to respond. As a response to this more knowledgeable, demanding customer, six shapers of today's—and tomorrow's—organizations have emerged.

Organization Shapers

These are the six organization shapers:

- Buyer power
- Variety and solutions
- The Internet
- Multiple dimensions
- Change
- Speed

Buyer Power

The new competition shifts power to the buyers, who know they are gaining power and learning how to use it. As a result, more organizational structures are being designed around customers or market segments. In addition, more initiatives are being launched to please customers, and as a result they too shape organizations.

Variety and Solutions

One response to buyer power is to increase the number of products and services offered and to customize them. To know more about customers, more and finer segments are created. The result is a greater variety and customization of offerings. To contend with this, management must know and understand more issues. Hence, it must collect more information, make more decisions, and set more priorities. As a result, management must bring more people into the decision processes. But customers do not want just a bundle of products and services. They want these products and services integrated into a solution for them. These customer solutions require cross-product coordination in addition to individual quality.

The Internet

Another shaper is the Internet. When a company does commerce over the Internet, its Web site becomes a single face to the customer. Sales forces, service personnel, call centers, and other customer touch points must coordinate their behavior in dealing with the customer. Separate processes for separate functions are no longer acceptable. The Internet is an inherently integrating force. The company's talent must be similarly integrated. Organizational units that never coordinated their activities must find ways to produce integrated responses to customers and suppliers.

Multiple Dimensions

Originally companies were single product or service entities organized around functions (Chandler, 1962). Starting in the 1920s companies led by General Motors and DuPont diversified into multiple product lines and then organized into multiple product divisions, each of which was a functional organization. In the 1960s, these companies expanded across borders and added an international division. Today, in addition to functions, products, and geography, companies must be organized by customer segments, solutions or offerings, and channels and processes. The complexity of today's business world translates into complexity of the company's organizational design. It is not possible to decentralize into nice, small autonomous business units. More complex networks across businesses and countries are now needed. There are more dimensions to be considered in making decisions.

Change

But no sooner is a decision made than the situation changes, requiring that management relearn and redecide. The combination of variety, multiple dimensions, and change causes the company to make still more decisions, more frequently. It needs to expand its decision-making capacity. This capacity is again expanded by including more people through decentralization but also through cross-departmental networks.

Speed

Customers not only want more variety and more comprehensive solutions than they used to, they also want them faster. In responding more quickly to customer requests, companies discover that they can benefit from additional efficiencies. With shorter lead times and cycle times, a company invests less in inventory and turns it more quickly. With these clear benefits to all parties, speed is the name of the game today. Speed also means that decisions must be moved to points of direct contact with the work. Thus speed too is a force for decentralization.

Today's organizations must be responsive and flexible. The necessary business strategies require state-of-the-art organizations. But it is very difficult to create state-of-the-art organizations. Like most difficult issues, such decisions land on the desk (or find their way into the e-mail in-box) of the chief executive. Chief executives, like it or not, are being forced to become involved in organizational design, first to create knowledge-based organizations, second to create effective, rapid responses to powerful customers, and third to integrate talent around the Internet and multiple dimensions.

Organization Design and Executive Leadership

Organization design decisions are landing on the chief executive's desk because they are difficult, priority issues. And the chief executives are getting involved because they see the decisions as high-leverage, and they see effective organization design as a source of competitive advantage in a world of temporary advantage.

Organization design decisions significantly affect the executive's unit. By choosing *who* decides and by designing the processes influencing *how* things are decided, the executive shapes every decision made in the unit. The leader becomes less of a *decision maker* and more of a *decision shaper*. Organization design decisions are the shapers of the organization's decision-making process.

Unique Organization Design

Organization designs that facilitate variety, change, speed, and integration are sources of competitive advantage. These designs are difficult to execute and copy because they are intricate blends of many different design policies. Thus they are likely to be sustainable sources of advantage.

A good example of competitive organization design is the 3M

Company. Although it has slipped in recent years, 3M has maintained an enviable record of entrepreneurship and new business development—despite being a hundred years old. Many outsiders have visited and observed 3M in action, but few have been able to duplicate its ability to create innovative new products. They can copy particular practices—for example, people at 3M spend 15 percent of their time on projects of their own choosing. But what makes the company's advantage sustainable is its unique blend of practices, values, autonomous structures, funding processes, rewards, and selection and development of product champions (Galbraith, 1982). That is difficult to copy; it is a competitive advantage for 3M. Similarly, all the automobile companies have been working for the last twenty years to copy the Toyota Production System. Yet they still cannot match the unique blend of policies that have been mastered by Toyota. Chapter Two of this volume lays out the framework for designing such intricate blends of organizational policies.

Balanced Perspective

The business world has changed. The solutions to many of today's issues have their roots in new organization designs. This new priority of organizing is easy to notice. It has been featured in cover articles in the business press, which has introduced us to the "horizontal organization," the "virtual corporation," the "modular organization," and so on. All this coverage indicates the new priorities—as well as an exceptional amount of hype.

The hype results in an overselling of some credible ideas. For example, it may lead some people to believe that such concepts as *teamwork* or *reengineering* are universal solutions rather than tools to be placed in the tool kit and taken out under the appropriate circumstances. Or the hype may desensitize people from ever listening to proposals for new organization practices with potential. I would like to take a more balanced approach, weighing the positives and negatives of current organization design alternatives.

I see the choice of organization as a design issue. The design of organizations is much like the design of other things—buildings, airplanes, computers. For example, everyone wants a lightweight laptop computer that is fast and doesn't cost much, and that has a large, clear color screen, lots of memory, a long battery life, and so on. Unfortunately, a computer cannot be designed that meets all of these criteria simultaneously. Trade-offs must be made. The computer designer must know which criteria are most important. By the same reasoning we cannot design simple organizations that provide a variety of products to a variety of customers on short cycle times and also capture economies of scale to provide low cost. Again, trade-offs must be made. The business strategy should set the criteria necessary for determining the priority task to accomplish. An organization can then be designed to meet those criteria. As a result, any organization is good at executing some activities but not good at others. The leader's task is to help the organization choose. This choice is the trade-off decision.

Any organization design has positives and negatives involved in every choice. The hype usually glosses over the negatives. Leaders who understand their organizations can articulate the negatives as well as the positives of their organizations. This understanding is important not only for choosing the appropriate organization but also for positioning the leader. The negatives are what the leader will have to manage. When every design choice has both positive and negative aspects, the selection of organization design will ultimately depend on the business strategy that the organization is to execute.

2

Choosing an Effective Design

The framework for organization design is the foundation on which a company bases its design choices. The framework consists of a series of design policies that is controllable by management and can influence employee behavior. The policies are the tools with which management must become skilled in order to shape the decisions and behaviors of their organizations effectively.

The Star Model

The organization design framework portrayed in Figure 2.1 is called the "star model." In the star model, design policies fall into five categories. The first is *strategy*, which determines direction. The second is *structure*, which determines the location of decision-making power. The third is *processes*, which have to do with the flow of information; they are the means of responding to information technologies. The fourth is *rewards* and reward systems, which influence the motivation of people to perform and address organizational goals. And the fifth category of the model is made up of policies relating to *people* (human resource policies), which influence and frequently define the employees' mind-sets and skills.

This book focuses primarily on structure and process policies and on matching appropriate combinations of them with the business strategy. The other design policies are vital and integral to the

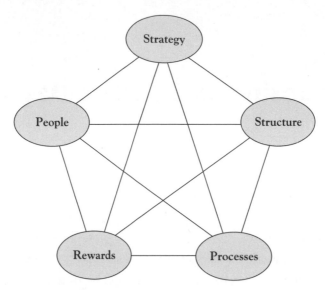

FIGURE 2.1. The Star Model.

whole organization and will be woven into the discussion when possible, but the reader is referred to other sources for an in-depth analysis of them (for example, see Mohrman, Galbraith, and Lawler, 1998). To provide a working familiarity with the five policy areas, general descriptions follow.

Strategy

Strategy is the company's formula for winning. The company's strategy specifies the goals and objectives to be achieved as well as the values and missions to be pursued; it sets out the basic direction of the company. The strategy specifically delineates the products or services to be provided, the markets to be served, and the value to be offered to the customer. It also specifies sources of competitive advantage and strives to provide superior value.

Traditionally, strategy is the first component of the star model to be addressed. It is important in the organization design process because it establishes the criteria for choosing among alternative organizational forms. Each organizational form enables some activities to be performed well while hindering others. Choosing organizational alternatives inevitably involves making trade-offs. Strategy dictates which activities are most necessary, thereby providing the basis for making the best trade-offs in the organization design.

Structure

The structure of the organization determines the placement of power and authority in the organization. Structure policies fall into four areas:

- Specialization
- Shape
- Distribution of power
- Departmentalization

Specialization refers to the type and numbers of job specialties used in performing the work. *Shape* refers to the number of people constituting the departments (that is, the span of control) at each level of the structure. Large numbers of people in each department create flat organization structures with few levels. *Distribution of power*, in its vertical dimension, refers to the classic issues of centralization or decentralization. In its lateral dimension, it refers to the movement of power to the department dealing directly with the issues critical to its mission. *Departmentalization* is the basis for forming departments at each level of the structure. The standard dimensions on which departments are formed are functions, products, work flow processes, markets, and geography. These five dimensions will be discussed in depth in Chapter Three.

Processes

Information and decision processes cut across the organization's structure; if structure is thought of as the anatomy of the

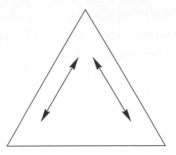

FIGURE 2.2. Vertical Processes.

organization, processes are its physiology or functioning. Management processes are both vertical and horizontal.

Vertical processes, as shown in Figure 2.2, allocate the scarce resources of funds and talent. Vertical processes are usually business planning and budgeting processes. The needs of different departments are centrally collected, and priorities are decided for the budgeting and allocation of the resources to capital, research and development, training, and so on.

Horizontal—also known as lateral—processes, as shown in Figure 2.3, are designed around the work flow—for example, new product development or the entry or fulfillment of a customer order. These management processes are becoming the primary vehicle for managing in today's organizations. Lateral processes can be carried out in a range of ways, from voluntary contacts between members to complex and formally supervised teams. (Chapters Four and Five focus on lateral processes.)

Rewards

The purpose of the reward system is to align the goals of the employee with the goals of the organization. It provides motivation and incentive for the completion of the strategic direction. The organization's reward system defines policies regulating salaries, promotions, bonuses, profit sharing, stock options, and so forth. A great

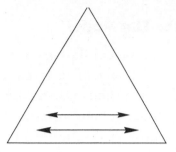

FIGURE 2.3. Lateral Processes.

deal of change is taking place in this area, particularly as it supports the lateral processes. Companies are now implementing pay-for-skill salary practices, along with team bonuses or gain-sharing systems. There is also the burgeoning practice of offering nonmonetary rewards such as recognition or challenging assignments.

The star model suggests that the reward system must be congruent with the structure and processes to influence the strategic direction. Reward systems are effective only when they form a consistent package in combination with the other design choices.

People

This area governs the human resource policies of recruiting, selection, rotation, training, and development. Human resource policies—in the appropriate combinations—produce the talent required by the strategy and structure of the organization, generating the skills and mind-sets necessary to implement its chosen direction. Like the policy choices in the other areas, these policies work best when consistent with the other connecting design areas.

Human resource policies also build the organizational capabilities to execute the strategic direction. Flexible organizations require flexible people. Cross-functional teams require people who are generalists and who can cooperate with each other. Human resource policies simultaneously develop people and organizational capabilities.

Implications of the Star Model

As the layout of the star model illustrates, structure is only one facet of an organization's design. This is important—most design efforts invest far too much time drawing the organization chart and far too little on processes and rewards. Structure is usually overemphasized because it affects status and power, and it is most likely to be reported in the business press. However, in a fast-changing business environment, structure is becoming less important, while processes, rewards, and people are becoming more important.

Another insight to be gained from the star model is that different strategies lead to different organizations. Although this seems obvious, it has ramifications that are often overlooked. There is no one-size-fits-all organization design that all companies—regardless of their particular strategy needs—should subscribe to. There will always be a current design that has become "all the rage." But no matter the fashionable design—whether it is the matrix design or the virtual corporation—trendiness is not sufficient reason to adopt an organization design. All designs have merit but not for all companies in all circumstances. The design—or combination of designs—that should be chosen is the one that best meets the criteria derived from the strategy.

A third implication of the star model is in the interweaving nature of the lines that form the star shape. For an organization to be effective, all the policies must be aligned, interacting harmoniously with one other. An alignment of all the policies will communicate a clear, consistent message to the company's employees.

The star model consists of policies that leaders can control and that can affect employee behavior, as suggested in Figure 2.4. It shows that managers can influence performance and culture —but only by acting through the design policies that affect behavior.

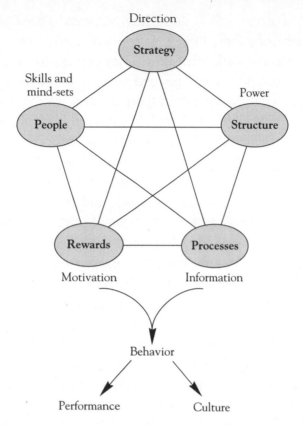

FIGURE 2.4. How Organization Design Affects Behavior.

Overcoming Negatives Through Design

One of the uses of the star model is to help overcome the negatives of any structural design. That is, every organization structure option has positives and negatives associated with it. If management can identify the negatives of its preferred option, the other policies around the star model can be designed to counter the negatives while achieving the positives.

Centralization can be used as an example. When the Internet became popular, many units in some organizations began their own initiatives to respond to it. These organizations experienced the positives of decentralization. They achieved speed of action, involvement of people closest to the work, and tailoring of the application to the work of the unit. They also experienced the negatives of decentralization. The many initiatives duplicated efforts and fragmented the company's response. There were multiple interfaces for customers and suppliers. They ran into difficulty in attracting talent and sometimes had to settle for less than top people.

Most companies responded by centralizing the activities surrounding the Internet into a single unit. In so doing, they reduced duplication, achieved scale economies, and presented one face to the customer. They combined many small Internet units into one large one, which made the job attractive for professional Internet managers. But at the same time, they moved decision making further from the work, the central unit became an internal monopoly, and the result could be lack of responsiveness to other organizational departments using the Internet.

To minimize the negatives of the central unit, the management of the company can design the appropriate processes, rewards, and staffing policies. For example, in the planning process, the central unit can present its plan to serve the rest of the organization. The leadership team can debate the plan and arrive at an approved level of service. The plan can be prepared by people from the central unit and a horizontal team of people from throughout the company. Along with its goals of reducing duplication and achieving scale, the central unit will also be expected to meet the planned service levels that were agreed on. The central unit's performance will be measured and rewarded on the basis of meeting planned goals. And finally, to keep the central unit connected to the work, it can be staffed by a mix of permanent professionals and rotating managers from the rest of organization on one- or two-year assignments. This complete design increases the chances that the central unit will achieve its positives while minimizing the usual negatives.

3

Matching Strategy and Structure

Once the strategy is established, the structure of the organization sets the framework for the other organization design decisions. The traditional hierarchical structure of organizations—with its dysfunctional effects—continues to fall under harsher and harsher criticism. At the same time, more and more structural design alternatives have begun to appear. There is an appropriate trend away from authoritarian management styles and the separatist titles and privileges of a multilevel hierarchy. Most companies have fewer hierarchical levels. Automation and information technology permit wider spans and therefore flatter structures (fewer hierarchical levels).

The Dimensions of Structure

Hierarchies, albeit flatter ones, will still be around for some time. They are useful for reaching decisions among large numbers of people in a timely fashion. They provide a basis for an appeals process for conflict resolution. But they are being implemented much more sparingly and in conjunction with alternative structures. Before we turn our attention to these alternatives, it is important to become familiar with the four policy areas that determine the structure of an organization. These policy areas, or dimensions, are the following:

- Specialization
- Shape
- Distribution of power
- Departmentalization

These policy areas are not listed in order of importance. Rather, departmentalization—with its far-reaching ramifications and attendant complexities—is saved for last.

Specialization

Specialization refers to the types and numbers of specialties to be used in performing the work. In general, the greater the number of specialties, the better the subtask performance. But specialization also makes it difficult to integrate subtasks into the performance of the whole task. Today, the trend is toward less specialization and more job rotation in low- to moderate-skill tasks in order to allow speed and ease of coordination, while in high-skill tasks the trend is toward greater specialization in order to allow pursuit of in-depth knowledge.

The old rules of the division of labor were to break tasks into subtasks and have people specialize in small pieces of the work. For complex tasks, the work could be divided so that an expert could bring in-depth knowledge to bear on difficult issues. Electrical engineering work was broken into electromechanical and electronics segments. The electronics segment could be further divided, down to the role of circuit designer for digital signal processing.

A different logic applied to the subdivision of low-skill tasks. Work was divided to create simple tasks so that uneducated workers could perform them at low wages. Such workers were easy to find and little training was needed. If turnover was high, new workers could be found and made productive at little expense. This thinking still applies in developing countries.

But in developed countries, the old logic applies only for complex, high-technology work. Companies in electronics, genetics, and pharmaceuticals all search for experts in specialized fields to push the limits of technology. The level of specialization is actually increasing as new specialties are created every day. Specialization of high-skill workers allows talented employees to gain greater expertise in their specific areas. The expertise can often be accumulated into databases and delivered to the teams by new information devices. These devices provide text, graphics, photos, and video to teach multiskilled workers. Thus, the expertise not only serves its primary purpose of allowing the specialist to gain in-depth knowledge but also can be disseminated to educate and inform generalists.

In contrast, at the low- and medium-skill levels, several forces are combining to eliminate highly fragmented tasks. Simple low-skill tasks are being automated (machines can do the tasks more cheaply and reliably than people can) or exported to developing countries. In addition, the costs of coordinating fragmented, inter-dependent tasks are too high in rapidly changing situations; a large amount of communication is needed to combine the work when hundreds of subtasks are involved. The remaining low- and moderate-skill work is being handled by multiskilled teams of educated workers. These teams are given end-to-end responsibility to make decisions for an entire piece of work, providing a more rapid and effective work flow.

These new work arrangements offer the benefits of greater speed and motivation and lower coordination costs (see Lawler, 1996).

Shape

Shape is determined by the number of people forming departments at each hierarchical level. The more people per department, the fewer the levels. The number of people in a department is usually referred to as the *span of control*—or span of supervision—of the department manager.

The trend today is to wider spans and flatter structures, as shown in Figure 3.1. As we move away from command-and-control

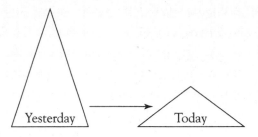

FIGURE 3.1. Trends in Organization Shape.

styles of leadership, managers can lead larger numbers. Thus the hierarchy becomes flatter. Fewer people are needed to supervise others. The flatter hierarchies lead to faster decisions, leaders who are in touch with organizational members, and lower overhead costs. But what is the best number for leaders to be able to provide help and training and make judgments about the work?

The Conference Board, a group that conducts research on organization structures, recently conducted a survey of spans of supervision among its members. With thousands of observations from work groups, the distribution ranged from 0 to 127 people. The distribution was trimodal, with modes at 7, 17, and 75. (The *mode*—as distinguished from *mean* and *median* as descriptors of central tendency—is the value that occurs most frequently. In this case, three numbers frequently occurred; hence, there was a trimodal distribution.) How could this happen?

The traditional organizational model typically used spans of about seven people (and a number of companies still do so). To communicate with subordinates and evaluate them, managers had the time for only about seven people. The traditional span can be increased or decreased based on several factors.

- The leader and group members are all experienced (so less communication and coaching are needed).
- Employees all do the same work.

- Each employee's task is independent of the others.
- The task is easily measured.

Thus groups of salespeople may include fifteen to twenty people while software design groups may consist of only five.

Delegation of work by the leader to the group also results in wider spans. Indeed, some organizations widen spans to encourage more delegation. Some organizations today monitor spans in organizational units and set goals to widen them progressively. They train their managers to adopt more of a coaching style and less of a controlling style. So spans of about seventeen are very possible.

A different kind of organization is needed for spans of seventy-five people. An example is a factory with a plant manager and seventy-five blue-collar workers. The workers are organized into three teams of twenty-five people, with a team for each of the three shifts. Each team is self-managing. It selects, trains, disciplines, and rewards all its own members. The teams schedule the work and propose capital investments. The plant manager advises the teams and spends most of the working day communicating with people outside the plant. Thus the more the managerial work is delegated to work teams, the less the need for direct supervision. These kinds of teams lead to the elimination of levels of supervision and the complete elimination of command-and-control styles.

In sum, it is quite possible to observe companies following the traditional management model, choosing spans of about seven. More delegation and goal setting can lead to spans of around seventeen. For companies with policies of self-managing teams, spans of around seventy-five are possible. It is important to follow all the policies on the star model to create these teams (see Lawler, 1996).

When looking at the shape of an organization with the purpose of creating a flatter structure, the spans of supervision, rather than hierarchical levels, are examined. This is because spans are more easily analyzed and changed; it is harder to eliminate levels. The redundant level may be different in different departments: the first level may be easiest to eliminate in one function, the third level easiest in another. Span analysis would lead to a reduction of levels and would account for differences among departments. So when reducing levels, an approach that widens spans is easier to implement than one that focuses on levels.

Distribution of Power

Distribution of power in an organization refers to two concepts. The first is the vertical distribution of decision-making power and authority. This is called *centralization* or *decentralization*. As illustrated in Chapter Two, there are pros and cons attached to changes in centralization. These should be weighed and tested against the strategy when choosing. The second concept is the horizontal distribution of power. The leader needs to shift power to the department dealing with mission-critical issues. Today in many competitive industries, the power to influence prices or terms and conditions is shifting to the knowledgeable customer. So inside the organization, the decision-making power is shifting to units with direct customer contact. In industries where contracting out has raised purchased goods and services to 80 percent of cost of goods sold, the purchasing function is being given increased decision-making power. A task of the leader is to weigh the business situation continuously and tilt the balance of power when change is required.

Departmentalization

The activities of organizations involving more than two dozen people are grouped together to form departments. *Departmentalization* refers to the choice of departments to integrate the specialized work and form a hierarchy of departments. The choice of type of department is made at each hierarchical level. Departments are usually formed to include people working in one of the following areas:

- A function or specialty
- A product line

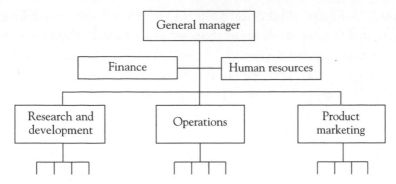

FIGURE 3.2. Functional Organization Structure.

- A customer segment
- A geographical area
- A work flow process

Each department type is appropriate for certain situations. The strategy and the size of the organization determines the choice.

Functional Structures. Most companies start by organizing around activities or functions. Companies of modest size usually adopt the functional structure shown in Figure 3.2. The diagram shows a typical Hewlett-Packard division.

The functional organization provides several advantages. First, gathering together all workers of one type—the R&D people, for example—allows them to transfer ideas, knowledge, and contacts among themselves. Second, it allows them to achieve a greater level of specialization. When two hundred or so engineers are pooled, they can afford to dedicate some to such specialties as circuit designers for gallium arsenide semiconductors. Third, using the example of a single purchasing function in operations, pooling the workers allows the company to present a single face to vendors and exercise buying leverage. Fourth, taking the example of using one manufacturing function to perform all production work, the company can afford to buy an expensive piece of test equipment and share it across product lines. Thus the functional structure permits more scale and specialization than other structural alternatives for companies of a certain size.

Organizations with functional departments also promote standardization and reduce duplication. An activity that is organized functionally is performed in the same way and (presumably) in the best way throughout the company. The functions adopt one system or one policy for everyone rather than have each department invent its own. The functions adopt a single computer system, inventory control policy, absenteeism policy, and so on. Companies often revert to the functional structure to reduce the proliferation and duplication of systems, standards, and policies that result when independent units don't manage to share or cooperate.

The functional organization has two weaknesses that frequently lead to the adoption of alternative structures. The first becomes apparent if a company has a variety of products, services, channels, and customers. The situation is illustrated in Figure 3.3. Apple Computer used the functional organization to great advantage when it produced only Macintosh computers and sold them through computer dealers. However, the product line expanded to include desktops, laptops, and palmtops, and the sales channels expanded to include direct sales, direct marketing, and mass merchandisers as well as computer dealers. This kind of variety overwhelms the decision-making capacity of the general manager and the functional leadership team. Thus Apple, like other companies in similar situations, abandoned the single functional structure. Interestingly, when Steve Jobs returned to Apple, he simplified the product lines and channels and brought back the functional structure.

The functional organization is best at managing a single product or service line. When strategies involve product or service diversification and market segmentation, the functional organization is either changed by organizing departments around products and markets or enhanced by introducing lateral processes. (The latter are described in Chapters Four and Five.)

The other weakness of the functional structure is the barriers

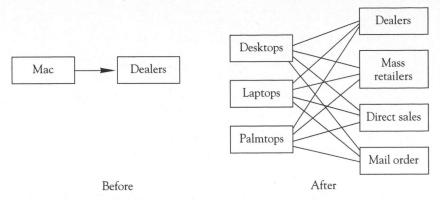

Before   After

FIGURE 3.3. Apple: Before and After Reorganization.

created between different functions, inhibiting cross-functional processes such as new product development. When a company has only one product line (which does not change often) and when long product development cycles are feasible, the functional organization can manage the cross-functional processes and simultaneously deliver scale, expertise, and efficiency. But mass customization, short product life cycles, and rapid product development times overwhelm the functional structure. Thus today this structure is being replaced by product, market, or process structures and by lateral cross-functional processes.

Thus the functional organization is appropriate for small companies and for those that need proprietary expertise and scale. It is appropriate if product and market variety is small, and if product life and development cycles are long. It is declining in popularity because in many industries speed is more important than scale, and responsiveness to variety from any source is a condition for survival.

Product Structures. The functional structure is usually superseded by a product structure. When a company diversifies its product lines and those lines achieve minimum efficient scale for their own manufacturing, the company creates multiple functional organizations, each with its own product line as illustrated in Figure 3.4.

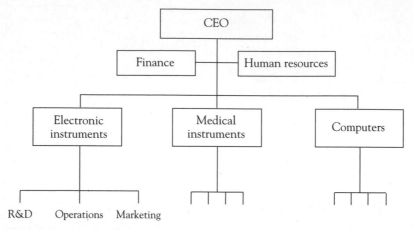

FIGURE 3.4. Product Structure.

Hewlett-Packard and 3M became famous for continually subdividing divisions and product lines when scale permitted. Each division focused on a single product line and new product development. Forming departments or divisions around products is the best way to compress the product development cycle. So product structures became the standard method for managing strategies of product diversification and new product development. To create a new product, management created a new division.

But product structures have their own weaknesses. Product general managers all want autonomy. Each product division then reinvents the wheel, duplicating resources and generally missing opportunities for sharing. These features are the strengths of the functional structure. Therefore, companies usually augment product structures with lateral functional processes, as discussed in Chapters Four and Five.

Another weakness of product structures is the possible loss of economies of scale. Not all functions can be divided into product units without a scale loss. These functions are often kept centralized and shared. This situation creates hybrid structures that are mostly product but have a central shared function.

At Boeing's commercial aircraft group, the design and manufacture of planes is divided into product lines of narrow bodies (737,

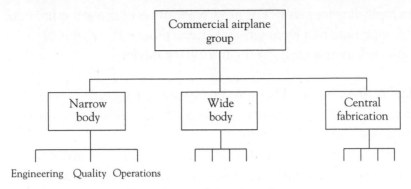

FIGURE 3.5. Hybrid Product and Function Structure.

757) and wide bodies (747, 767, and 777). However, the fabrication of major structural components requires very large and expensive computer-controlled machine tools. These would be too expensive to duplicate in each product line. Instead, a central fabrication unit is created and all manufacturing activities requiring scale and skill are placed in it and shared across product lines. The structure, shown in Figure 3.5, is a hybrid of products and functions. A similar situation can occur with the purchasing function. Today many companies are contracting out their component manufacturing. Purchased material can become as much as 80 percent of the cost of goods sold. In that situation, purchasing and procurement becomes an attractive candidate for a central shared function.

The biggest challenge to the product structure comes from customers who buy from more than one product division. In the past, a central sales function was created to handle all products. But today customers want sourcing relationships, solutions rather than stand-alone products, information exchange, a personalized Web site, single point of contact, and one invoice. These demands are forcing companies to create customer or market segment structures as a front end of the business to complement a product-focused back end. (The front/back model will be discussed in Chapter Seven.)

In summary, the product structure was, and in some cases still is, the organization structure of choice for manufacturing companies, allowing them to manage strategies of product diversification and rapid development. The negative features of this structure may be compensated for by functional lateral processes, by central functions, and, increasingly, by the front/back model.

Market Structures. The most rapidly increasing type of structure is the one based on customers, markets, or industries. There are several reasons for the popularity.

The first reason is the shift in power in many industries to the buyer. Increased global competition has created more capacity than demand in many industries, thereby giving the buyer more choices. The buyer is aware of the choice and is learning how to use this newfound buying power. In many cases, buyers are insisting on dedicated units to serve their needs.

Second, the decline of scale in manufacturing—combined with higher-volume, single-sourcing arrangements—makes it economical for a supplier to dedicate a unit to serve a customer. For example, 7-Eleven of Japan has chosen Ajinomoto as the sole supplier of some food products and given it a large volume of business. Ajinomoto, in return, has created a unit to manufacture and sell products exclusively to 7-Eleven stores in Japan.

Third, the shift to market structures is enabled by the increased trend toward and willingness to contract out. Previously, a function that required scale might have forced the company into a functional or hybrid structure. Today, if the scale function is not a source of competitive advantage, it can be contracted out. For example, recording companies can form labels around small, fast-moving market segment units that perform all functions and contract out the essential but not critical compact disc manufacturing. (Actually, contracting out could enable any of the nonfunctional structures to be adopted.)

Fourth, there is a shift of competitive advantage to those companies with superior knowledge and information about market segments. Inexpensive information technology, access to databases and networks, bar code data, a dedicated Web site like MyAmex.com at American Express, and so on, allow a company organized by market segment to gain superior knowledge about the preferences, buying habits, and lifestyles of customers in those segments. It can then create products and services that offer superior value to those customers. In the music business, a company usually organizes around market segments—classical, rock, country, rap, and so on. Recording companies create a label for each segment. The segment focuses on its customers and artists. The winners are the ones that attract the top talent and know the customers best.

The final reason for the increased popularity of the customer structure is the increasing proportion of service businesses in operation today. Service businesses usually focus on—and organize around—market segments. Services are usually customized and personalized for various segments of the population or industry. Banks, telecommunications firms like MCI, hotels like Marriott, and engineering and construction firms focus on market segments and industries for their divisions.

Market structures have negatives that are similar to those of product structures. Market divisions have a tendency to duplicate activities and develop incompatible systems. They may reduce scale if there is no contracting out. (Hybrid structures that centralize and share purchasing or central telecom networks, like the ones at the former regional Bell companies such as Verizon or SBC, can achieve market focus and efficient scale simultaneously.) They also have difficulty sharing common products or services, which may go to several market segments. Banks may provide a cash management service to customer segments based on their size, such as multinational firms, large corporations, and medium-size companies. Banks would like the segments to share the expensive cash management system bought by all segments and not duplicate it in each market unit.

Thus organizations structured upon market or customer divisions are the fastest-growing kind. Their popularity reflects their compatibility with increasing buyer power, sourcing arrangements, declining scale, contracting out, the shift to the service economy, and especially the increasing competitive advantage of superior market segment knowledge and information.

Geographical Structures. Geographical structures traditionally developed as companies expanded their offerings across territories. There was usually a need to be close to the customer and to minimize the costs of travel and distribution. Sometimes industries, like timber and coal, needed to locate near sources of supply. Today, the economics of location is important—but information technology is making it less important in certain industries. The use of geographical structure depends entirely on the industry.

In service industries where the service is provided on site, geography continues to be a structural basis for many companies. Service businesses and sales and service functions have always been geographically organized around districts, regions, and areas. McDonald's and Pizza Hut have geographical structures; the regions are influenced by span-of-control choices and the economics of distribution of food ingredients. Food service companies are likely to have flatter structures in the future, but they will still be geographical.

Geography is becoming less important in other sales and service activities. Sales forces and knowledge services—like consulting— were traditionally managed out of local offices, based on personal relationships and knowledge of the region. Relationships are still important, but industry knowledge and expertise are becoming more important: to sell to banks, one must be well-versed in the banking industry. As a result, industry or market segment structures are being adopted. Sales are also being made through electronic markets, direct computer access by a customer, 800 numbers, and catalogues. Selling today requires fewer office calls by expensive direct sales forces.

However, changes to the geographical structure are occurring in industries where the technology is creating smaller efficient scale and flexible plants and where customers demand just-in-time delivery. Functional organizations are being replaced by multiple small, fast profit centers. Smaller factories can be located close to the customer and produce a variety of products to serve all the needs of their customers. For example, Frito-Lay moved to a geographical structure recently. The company capitalizes on information captured by bar code scanners to move product with limited shelf life rapidly and frequently, and to move quickly on promotions.

The role of geography in manufacturing is complex, with a relationship between the ratio of product value to transport cost, and attention to the minimum efficient scale of a factory. Cement and paper are low-cost commodities with high transport costs. Such companies use regional profit centers. In contrast, semiconductors and pharmaceuticals are high-value items with low transport costs. They are global products and geography is less important and product more important in determining the organization structures of these firms.

Service companies that provide information and knowledge processing are increasingly becoming location-free. The engineering and construction industries can gain an edge with effective geographical structure. At an oil company's new Asian refinery, the initial high-skilled work is performed at the company's North American offices, where the leading design skills are located. Most of this work is located in Los Angeles, but the Calgary and Houston offices have excess capacity and need work. So some design activities are moved electronically to these offices and coordinated through a common computer system. At the completion of the high-level design, the work is beamed over satellite to a group of three hundred Filipino engineers. They generate the fifteen thousand drawings to guide the construction work. This lower-skilled work is more cost effective when performed in the Philippines at Filipino wages.

Companies are seeking the best global location because they can move the work anywhere. Insurance companies send claims forms overnight to Ireland to be processed and returned by satellite the next day. With the new information technology, much service work can be moved anywhere in this way, creating the location-free organization.

Many other service activities are becoming location-free. The elevator business was one in which companies made their money on the service contract and spare parts. A worldwide, geographically structured service organization was a competitive advantage. However, things have changed; today, elevators are designed not to fail. Electronic components mean fewer moving parts and less need for timely, nearby service calls. There is also a large component of software in elevator controls, which can be monitored and repaired from any remote location. Sensors can be installed in critical areas of potential failure. When monitors at a remote location report a likely failure, repair crews can be dispatched from their bases. The monitoring and repair crews can be located in the most cost-effective areas of the world, provided those locations have skilled people and good telecom and airport infrastructures. In the future, as distance learning and remote medicine become feasible and popular, education and health will likewise become less location based.

Process Structures.   The newest generic organization structure is the process structure. There is considerable variation in what people are calling a process organization, however. In general, a process structure is based on a complete flow of work, such as that of the order fulfillment process. This process flows from initiation by a customer order through the functions to delivery to the customer. Currently, each function performs a part of the work along the sequential flow. The advocates of the process organization—sometimes also called the horizontal organization—suggest that the people from each function who work on the process should be gathered into a process team and given end-to-end responsibility for the overall process. The process team reports to a process leader. The structure is thereby converted from a vertical functional structure to a horizontal process structure, as shown in Figure 3.6.

The process structure is the culmination of three strategic initiatives that all focused on work flow processes and fought against the barriers of the functional structure. The first was total quality (TQ). TQ efforts all promote understanding processes, controlling processes, and improving processes to meet criteria defined by the customer. Cross-functional coordination is essential. The second

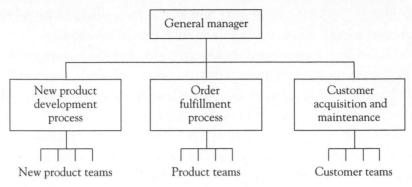

FIGURE 3.6. Process Organization Structure.

initiative was cycle-time reduction. The attainment of speed requires tight coordination across functions. Finally, reengineering brought the new information technology to bear on the redesign of the processes themselves. Clearly, the momentum for a process orientation has been building for some time.

The process structure has been offered as an alternative to the functional structure. And there is much to recommend it. Perhaps the greatest benefit is a fresh look, from end to end, at the whole process. When combined with new information technologies, there is considerable opportunity for redesign of an entire process. A change in one function's piece may make an enormous difference in the pieces of the other functions. By having one manager in charge of the whole process rather than individual managers for each function, the resistance to process change can be overcome.

A process with end-to-end coverage also lends itself to measurement more easily than a group of functions does. Each function is responsible for a piece of the process. A unit responsible for the entire process is responsible for a reasonably self-contained piece of work. The unit can control most of the variables that influence the performance of the process. Hence, the unit can be held accountable.

A process orientation leads to cycle-time reduction by doing a good job of coordinating work across functions. Thus companies competing on time-to-market and fast-delivery bases will find a process organization far superior to a functional structure.

In addition, some costs are reduced with a process organization. The faster time cycles mean reduced inventories and faster receipt of cash. The reduced working capital translates into reduced costs of carrying inventory and cash. Other costs are reduced because duplication of work across functions is eliminated. With a functional structure, often one division will not trust the input of another and will check and rework information to its own satisfaction. A process organization eliminates such redundant activities, verifying input once for all functions.

The process organization is therefore superior to the functional organization in businesses with short product life and development cycles. It is also superior when the redesign of processes has great potential for reducing costs and satisfying the customer. In contrast, the functional organization is superior for companies with long cycles and where scale and expertise are important. Yet the benefits of a process orientation can still be obtained by creating lateral process teams that coordinate across the functional structure.

When compared with the functional organization, the process organization can break down barriers and achieve significant savings. However, the structure should be adopted with care. It is currently fashionable, which means the weaknesses associated with it get suppressed. When compared with product or market segment structures, it is not yet clear how the process structure stacks up. Product and market structures have themselves knocked down functional barriers and achieved end-to-end focus on products and customers. And the process structure creates its own barriers—for example, a handoff between the new product process group and the order fulfillment process group, as a product moves from new to existing status. In contrast, the product organization would be seamless on this issue.

The permanent process organization seems to be disappearing. Companies like Cisco have automated processes like order entry and moved them to the Web. There are no people involved. So as process activities move into software and the software process moves to the Web and is even outsourced, the need for permanent process structures disappears. However, a strong process team is needed to design the process before it is automated. This team is a temporary process structure.

Ultimately, combining a process focus within a product or market structure should prove to be a powerful productivity enhancer. It is probable that product, market, or geographical divisions will be the basic profit centers. The subunits within these profit centers will be divided into functions or processes that are useful within product or customer structures.

Choosing Structures

The leader's first organization design choice is the basic structure. This choice process begins with an understanding of the business's strategy. By matching what is required by the strategy to what is done best by the various structures, the leader can optimize the decision. The kinds of strategies executed best by the basic structures are listed as follows:

Functional Structure

- Small-size, single-product line
- Undifferentiated market
- Scale or expertise within the function
- Long product development and life cycles
- Common standards

Product Structure

- Product focus
- Multiple products for separate customers

- Short product development and life cycle
- Minimum efficient scale for functions or outsourcing

Market Structure

- Important market segments
- Product or service unique to segment
- Buyer strength
- Customer knowledge advantage
- Rapid customer service and product cycles
- Minimum efficient scale in functions or outsourcing

Geographical Structure

- Low value-to-transport cost ratio
- Service delivery on site
- Closeness to customer for delivery or support
- Perception of the organization as local
- Geographical market segments needed

Process Structure

- Best seen as an alternative to the functional structure
- Potential for new processes and radical change to processes
- Reduced working capital
- Need for reducing process cycle times

Unfortunately, in the typical situation no one type of structure best fits the business strategy. The decision maker should list the strengths and weaknesses of each structural alternative. The decision maker must also develop priorities for strategic attributes, such as cycle-time reduction or scale of manufacturing. Then the choice of structure can be made for the top priorities. The structural alternatives that are runners-up become candidates for hybrid structures or for lateral coordination processes.

Although the traditional hierarchy is losing favor, flatter hierarchies will be with us for some time. The functional, product, market, geographical, and process alternatives all have their own strengths and weaknesses. For some structures, the weaknesses can be overcome with hybrid structures. For others, lateral processes can augment the basic structures. Indeed, to be responsive on multiple dimensions, lateral processes are key. These processes will be discussed in the next two chapters.

4

Linking Processes to Coordination Needs

Most of the activity in an organization does not follow the vertical hierarchical structure. As continuous change becomes the natural state in most industries, lateral processes become the principal means of coordinating activities.

Lateral processes are information and decision processes that coordinate activities spread out across different organizational units, providing mechanisms for decentralizing general management decisions. They accomplish the decentralization by recreating the organization in microcosm for the issue at hand. That is, each department with information about—and a stake in—an issue contributes a representative for issue resolution, as shown in Figure 4.1.

No matter what type of hierarchical structure is chosen, many activities will require coordination across departments. Most organizations deal with a complex world. They have to do business with multiple customers, multiple partners, multiple suppliers. They have to compete with rivals in many areas of the world. They deal with governments, regulators, distributors, labor unions, and trade associations. They employ different skill specialties and use multiple technologies while producing a variety of products and services. If a company creates an organization to maximize its effectiveness in dealing with one constituency—for example, customers—it fragments its ability to deal with others—for example, unions. All the

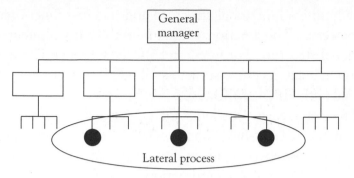

FIGURE 4.1. Lateral Processes Across Departments.

Source: Galbraith, J., *Competing with Flexible Lateral Organizations, 2/E,* © 1994, p. 6. Reprinted/adapted by permission of Pearson Education, Inc., Upper Saddle River, New Jersey.

dimensions not handled by the structure require coordination through lateral management processes.

Today, these other dimensions are increasing in number and importance. In addition to focusing on more powerful and knowledgeable customers, a company must leverage its own buying power, concentrate its R&D investments on its leading technologies and core competencies, and become a good citizen in regions where active host governments negotiate relationships. Companies must focus simultaneously on governments, customers, functions, vendors, and products. Lateral processes are designed to provide the company with the networks and capability of addressing all these concerns. Today a company must create a multidimensional organization built around its basic structure. A company must be flexible in addressing whatever unpredictable issue arises, whether it presents a threat or an opportunity.

Lateral Coordination

The organization designer must match the amount of lateral coordination needed to execute a multidimensional strategy with different types and amounts of lateral processes. To learn how to match coordination needs and lateral processes, let us examine a single-business functional structure and its cross-functional lateral processes. The functional structure is the most common organizational structure. For more on this, see Chapter Three. For a discussion of lateral processes across subsidiaries and business units, see Galbraith (1994, 2000).

The management challenge for a functional organization is to coordinate the cross-functional work flows and common contact points with customers, suppliers, and other shared constituencies as indicated in Figure 4.2. Coordination across functions—to create and deliver products or services—is the responsibility of the general manager and the functional management team. As mentioned in Chapter Three, this coordination is most easily accomplished when the company produces a single line of products or services for a single customer type, and when product life and development cycles are long.

But the need for lateral coordination will exceed the capacity of the team at the top when a company's strategies and tasks involve the following:

- Diversity
- Rapid change
- Interdependence between functional units
- Internet connections
- Speed

To deal with these forces, management may have to change the entire structure of an organization. But another alternative is to enlist lateral processes, which may be thought of as "general manager equivalents." These processes offer a different, more subtle approach to decentralizing decisions and increasing decision-making capacity. The types and amounts of lateral processes used will vary depending on the relative importance of the five forces.

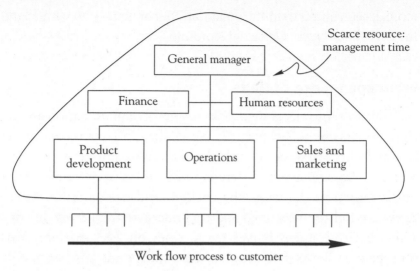

FIGURE 4.2. Work Flows Across Functional Structure.

Diversity

The more variety in a company's work, the more decentralization it needs. No functional management team can handle the priority setting required by multiple products in multiple markets. For example, Compaq has evolved from a company offering a single product sold through dealers in the United States to one offering many products sold through multiple channels domestically as well as in Europe, Asia, and Latin America. Its organization has developed from the simple functional form to more complex matrix designs and finally to the front/back model described later.

Rapid Change

Rapid change—when combined with diversity—overwhelms a functional management team. Management must make and remake decisions as situations change and new circumstances arise. Communication about new events is required. The organization managing a product with a rapid life cycle like that of rap music will be more decentralized than the organization managing one with a long life cycle like that of classical recordings.

Interdependence of Units

Execution of interdependent tasks requires communication among the task performers. Boeing's 777 project has 250 teams performing the work; an investment bank also has 250 teams performing its work. Boeing's teams are design-and-build teams for sections of the aircraft, such as the wing, the cockpit, and the avionics. These teams are tightly integrated and communicate frequently. In contrast, the investment bank's teams work on 250 separate deals for separate clients. Each team can act independently because its work will not affect the others. These teams are less interdependent. They require less cross-team coordination than the Boeing teams do.

Internet Connections

A special type of interdependence is being created by the migration of business processes to the Internet and to in-house intranets using the same technology. A few years ago the various groups at a consumer bank made independent contacts with a customer.

- A direct marketing group would mail promotions to customers for home equity loans.
- A call center would receive and reply to inquiries from a customer about a question or a dispute concerning their balances.
- A sales call center would initiate a promotion for investment funds on the customer's birthday.
- A "bank-by-phone" offering would allow the customer to make routine bill payments.
- The automatic teller machine (ATM) would allow the customer to perform other routine transactions.

- The tellers would interact with the customers on visits to branches for transactions.
- Salespeople in the branches or in the customer's home would propose a mortgage to the home buyer if requested.

Today most consumer financial services companies are installing Customer Relationship Management (CRM) software and putting it on their intranet. Now a customer's profile can appear on a screen before anyone interacts with that customer. The ultimate goal of the CRM process designers is to capture information about the customer at each customer touch point and integrate that information so as to better serve that customer. Then the various units should coordinate their contacts. For example, if a customer has lodged a product complaint with the call center and that complaint is unresolved, the marketing people do not want to send a promotion suggesting another product. This type of information was not practical before the development of Internet technology. But now the connected groups are interdependent. They need to coordinate their actions where before they did not and could not. The interdependence needs to be managed so as to serve the customer better by using the CRM process.

Speed

Finally, cycle-time reduction demands for new products, customer orders, and customer service requests substantially increase the need for cross-functional coordination. To accomplish these reductions, decisions must be moved to the points of product and customer contact; there simply is no time to go up the hierarchy to find a general manager. Lateral processes create a general manager equivalent at the point of action.

Thus collectively these five forces determine the need for cross-functional coordination and the correlating amount of cross-functional lateral processes. It is important to recognize that the need varies, from low (for companies manufacturing beer or producing classical music titles, for example) to high (for those producing multimedia products and rap music titles).

The Benefits and Costs of Lateral Processes

As noted, the task of the organization designer is to match the type and amount of lateral processes with the cross-functional coordination required by the firm's business strategy. The designer must avoid choosing too little or too much lateral processing. Up to a point, lateral processes produce benefits; thereafter, they increase costs and difficulty.

What are the benefits of lateral processes? The benefits involve permitting the company to make more decisions, different kinds of decisions, and better and faster decisions.

Because lateral processes decentralize general management decisions, they free up top management for other decisions. Thus they increase the capacity of the organization to make more decisions more often. The organization is therefore more adaptable to constant change. Different types of decisions are made and can address the multiple dimensions of a business environment. Companies decentralize choice to the points of product and customer contact where decisions can be made and implemented quickly because these groups may have access to current and local information available only to them.

A business may have a functional structure but, by enlisting lateral processes, it becomes capable of forming new product teams, customer teams, and process teams for reengineering. The business is therefore flexible, no matter the issue at hand.

However, lateral processes can also create costs. The decentralized decisions may not be better than those of top management. The people at the front lines may not have the perspective and experience of top management. These costs can be minimized, however, by making the organization's total database available, by training people, and providing the correct incentives.

Another cost comes in the form of the time of the people

involved. With today's flat and lean hierarchical structures, employee time is at a premium. Time spent on a reengineering team is time not spent with customers or developing new hires. The more time spent on teams, the greater the cost. Lateral processes can be seen as investments of management time to create shorter cycle times.

The third cost comes in increased level of conflict. Cross-functional teams are made up of representatives who see issues differently. Much of the time involved in cross-functional processes is devoted to communicating, problem solving, and resolving conflicts. The company that is skilled at conflict resolution can lower the costs and time needed to reach decisions.

Thus the designer needs to find the point of balance between the benefits and costs of lateral processes. This balance can be struck by matching coordination needs with the different types and amounts of lateral processes.

The Five Types of Lateral Processes

There are five basic types of lateral processes, as shown in Figure 4.3. They vary in the amount of management time and energy that must be invested in them.

Informal or *voluntary* lateral processes occur spontaneously. They are the least expensive and easiest form to use. Although they occur naturally, organization designers can greatly improve the frequency and effectiveness of these voluntary processes.

E-coordination involves using Internet technology to communicate and coordinate across departments. These electronic links may combine the efforts of people working on a new product using three-dimensional computer-aided design (3D-CAD) or serving the same customer using CRM processes.

The next type of lateral process, which requires more time commitment, is the *formal group*. Teams or task forces are formally created, members appointed, charters defined, and goals set for the cross-functional effort. Formal groups are more costly than voluntary

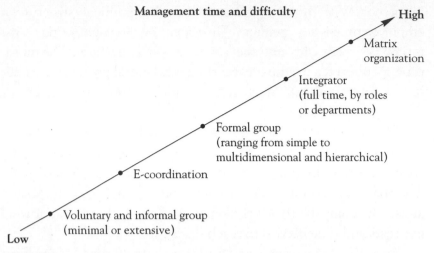

FIGURE 4.3. Types of Lateral Processes.

Source: Galbraith, J., *Competing with Flexible Lateral Organizations, 2/E,* © 1994. Reprinted/adapted by permission of Pearson Education, Inc., Upper Saddle River, New Jersey.

groups because they are the creation of management and do not occur naturally. They require some team building and maintenance for proper functioning.

Formal groups are also more costly because they are used in addition to the voluntary groups, not instead of them. The organization needs both voluntary efforts and formal groups to supplement the general manager's coordination across functions. The simpler forms are still needed but are insufficient by themselves to achieve the integration the strategy requires.

The fourth level of commitment to lateral processes comes with appointment of *integrators* to lead the formal groups. At some point, full-time leaders may be required. Leaders may be product managers, project managers, process managers, brand managers, and so on. They are all "little general managers," who manage a product or service in place of the general manager. They are enlisted because there are many products, new products, and rapid life cycles.

Using integrators is the most costly lateral process. In addition to the cumulative costs of the voluntary processes and the formal

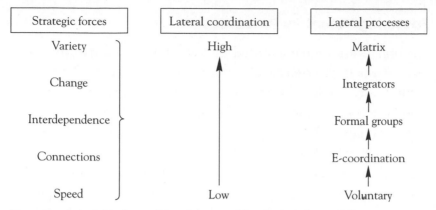

FIGURE 4.4. Matching Coordination Needs with Lateral Processes.

groups that must already be in place, integrators require hiring a group of full-time people whose task is to integrate the efforts of others. The integrator role is also the most difficult to execute. Integrators introduce confusion over roles and responsibilities and an element of conflict. However, the cost and difficulty may be judged appropriate because the strategy requires functional excellence and rapid generation of new products or services.

The last and most difficult form of lateral process is the *matrix organization*. To create a matrix, the integrator role becomes a line organizational position. The person in the functions who works on the products or project team acquires a second boss. The company then has two line organizations. The matrix is used only when there is a need for a power balance. The R&D function, for example, is typically organized around projects and functions in a matrix model.

The organization designer must match a company's cross-functional coordination requirements with the appropriate types and amounts of lateral processes. Figure 4.4 illustrates how the five strategic forces create a need for varying levels of lateral processes.

The remainder of this chapter describes how the organization designer can foster voluntary processes and e-coordination. The other types of lateral processes—formal groups, integrators, and matrix organizations—are discussed in depth in Chapter Five.

Fostering Voluntary Processes

An organization characterized by voluntary coordination across units is usually referred to as an informal organization. The process seems to occur naturally and spontaneously. For example, a discussion between a salesperson and a customer leads to an idea for a product change. The salesperson and an engineer make a preliminary design. The design is sent to operations and marketing for their ideas. A new product modification results a few weeks later, all because of the voluntary cooperation of people in different units.

Such acts may occur hundreds of times each day and can be a source of great strength for the company. But great weakness occurs when the voluntary acts do not happen. In many cases these acts do not occur because of cross-functional barriers.

Today there is great interest in removing barriers and encouraging voluntary cooperation. Leaders can employ a number of actions to elicit voluntary cooperation:

- Interdepartmental rotation
- Interdepartmental events
- Co-location
- Mirror image departments
- Consistent reward and measurement systems

All these forms of activity create networks of relationships. People cooperate voluntarily when they have relationships with people in other departments and are comfortable working with them.

Interdepartmental Rotation

The most powerful tool of the organization designer for creating voluntary lateral processes is the interdepartmental assignment of key people. Rotational assignments have two important effects. First, they train and develop people in all facets of the business.

People who are successful at rotational assignments learn how to learn, they do not simply gain the specific knowledge of the business. The rotated managers can more effectively participate in cross-functional teams. They can chair the teams and grow into integrators. Rotations create generalists and the general management capability that is at the heart of lateral processes. Individuals become more flexible—and if we are to create flexible organizations, we need flexible people. These people also develop relationships in the various departments, which then can be used later in lateral coordination attempts.

Thus rotational assignments create a lateral communication network across the company (see Galbraith, 1994, pp. 46–50). Taken together, the trained individuals and the relationships they have cultivated create the organizational capability for lateral coordination. Rotational experiences simultaneously develop the individuals and build their relationships, thereby developing the voluntary organization. The task of the organization designer is to make sure that relationships are created at key work flow interfaces where coordination is required.

However, rotations also create costs. People are less effective when they are learning new roles. When managers are reluctant to give up good people and train newcomers, effort and time from the leader is needed to keep the rotation process in motion. But the cost of rotations should realistically be considered an investment instead of an expense as it develops individuals, creates a network of relationships, and builds a flexible, lateral capability.

Interdepartmental Events

Voluntary processes also result from events such as training courses and conferences. Indeed, training budgets are as justified by their networking effects as by their developmental effects. The organization designer only needs to decide who should attend. Also, like rotational assignments, events are most effective when they create relationships across the key work flow interfaces.

The importance of training in strategy provides an opportunity for developing people and developing the organization's networks. When companies rely on informal, voluntary cooperation and e-coordination, the people need to know and participate in the creation of the company's strategy and priorities. Training in and participation in the strategy is a great way of preparing people with direct customer contact to know how to serve the customer appropriately.

Co-location

Proximity of employees is an important factor in fostering productive relationships. There is good evidence that reducing distance and physical barriers between people increases the amount of communication between them. Engineering firms co-locate everyone working on a project. As projects come and go, the firms reconfigure the organization and the office layouts.

The organization designer needs to give careful thought to location patterns. For example, if a marketing group is located close to an operations group perhaps it is not located close to engineering. Once again, the designer needs to know the key interfaces where communication is most necessary and relationships most likely to be productive.

Mirror Image Departments

One of the greatest barriers to lateral processes is the sheer number of interfaces across which people must communicate to gain a consensus for action. Usually, each function organizes according to its own logic. For example, in one consumer packaged goods company, over twenty interfaces would have to be worked for a salesperson and an engineer to modify a product. Sales is organized by geography, marketing by brands, manufacturing by site and process, engineering by product, purchasing by commodity and vendor. It would take an engineer an unrealistic

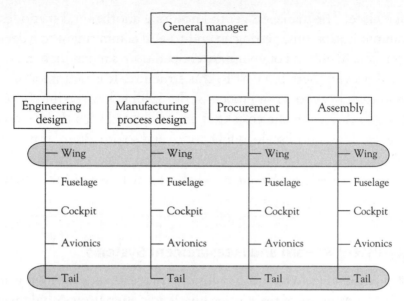

FIGURE 4.5. Mirror Image Functional Structure.

Source: Galbraith, J., *Competing with Flexible Lateral Organizations, 2/E,* © 1994. Reprinted/adapted by permission of Pearson Education, Inc., Upper Saddle River, New Jersey.

amount of time to communicate with and gain support from each function.

In response, some companies have organized their functions as mirror images of one another. Figure 4.5 shows how an airplane manufacturer has organized each function around major sections of the aircraft. A manager of the wing, for example, has an interface in each other function. Each person has to work only five or six interfaces in order to get complete support. These five or six people can form the equivalent of a general manager for the wing, tail, avionics, and so on. Decisions can be decentralized to these groups, with each group assuming end-to-end responsibility for its section of the aircraft. It is an easy next step to formalize the group and have it set group goals for cycle time, quality, and cost improvements.

The mirror image structure creates a clear line of sight across the entire organization. It can facilitate establishment of relationships by simplifying the interfaces across which lateral processes take place. The managers get to know one another and spend less communication time getting an end-to-end commitment to a decision. The likelihood of voluntary cooperation is much higher.

However, there is a cost to this structure. It is tantamount to organizing by product or process at the level below the functional manager. It creates the costs that are associated with those structures, such as loss of scale, duplication, and so on. Often, the costs are accepted in order to get the coordination and cycle-time reduction. Or the designer can create a hybrid structure within the function.

Consistent Reward and Measurement Systems

One of the keys to creating voluntary processes across units is to align the interests of the parties involved. Often, functional measurements designed independently of each other create incompatible goals, causing another barrier to cross-functional cooperation. A task of the leader is to test for cross-unit consistency of goals and to design supporting reward systems. Performance measurement and reward systems are useful tools for creating aligned goals and objectives. Often, a common goal, like cycle-time reduction, can apply across all functions. Or there may be a customer for the cross-functional work. The group can start with what the customer wants in order to generate measurement criteria. But in any case, clear and consistent measures, goals, and correlated rewards are needed to promote voluntary cooperation across units.

E-Coordination

The potential of Internet technology for linking previously independent departments is rapidly approaching realization. So far, individual functions have been moving their processes to the Web —we're seeing e-procurement, e-HR, Enterprise Resource Planning (ERP) systems, and CRM for customers. Today the discussion is about Enterprise Systems (ES), which is all about the integration of these functional islands. In the short run, the issues will be technical challenges around integrating HR applications from Peoplesoft with CRM applications from Siebel Systems. But the real challenge will be the integration of previously independent departments around supply chain processes and customer management processes. For this integration to happen, leadership needs skills in lateral processes to link the functions. Many of these will be voluntary or informal organizations facilitated by intranets.

E-Coordination with a Service Contract on the Web

International Service Systems (ISS) is the largest provider of cleaning, security, and catering services in Europe. Recently, ISS has been signing national and regional agreements with customers who outsource these services to it. In one national agreement a U.K. manufacturer has outsourced its cleaning to ISS at all of its U.K. sites. It is a customized agreement for cleaning. For example, the offices are to be cleaned every night with special attention to PCs and keyboards. The back hallways and fire escapes are cleaned once a month, but reception areas and conference rooms are to be cleaned on demand. This contract and its application to various sites is placed on the ISS Web site. It is accessible to the cleaning crews by handheld, wireless devices.

The cleaning crews check their assignments and the cleaning criteria that apply to the areas assigned to them. When an area is complete, a sign-off signal is sent and registered at the Web site. Any comments can be noted. The site supervisor and national account manager can observe whether all areas at all sites have been serviced. The next day the customer site managers register their satisfaction with ISS's performance and give the crews a score. The site supervisors' and account managers' bonuses are determined by this score.

The on-demand cleaning is also registered on the Web site. When a request is registered on the site, an alert is sent to the cell phone of the site supervisor, who calls the crews. Some crews are cross-trained to provide cleaning, catering, and security services so that there is a quick response capability. Other requests can be registered as well. For example, say Prince Charles and members of the press will visit the factory in South Hampton on Friday afternoon. The highest level of cleaning is needed on all areas of his tour. In this manner, the Web site coordinates the behavior of various crews at multiple sites throughout the day.

Customer Relationship Management Systems

The consumer bank mentioned earlier relies on people in several departments to serve the customer and to record customer information on the CRM system. The company and the people need to understand all the important touch points and decide on how to manage the customer in a consistent way across all of these touch points. Then all the people at the touch points need a complete, single picture of the customer that is accessible to all. All these employees need to think beyond their own function when dealing with a customer. They are not just answering a billing inquiry or taking a complaint. All interactions can lead to a sale, today or in the future. So in addition to the CRM software, there is a need for training the people in the software and in customer management techniques.

Many new opportunities arise from the CRM data. When someone calls and inquires about their account balance, it is useful to see if they have visited a branch lately or made a deposit. A customer who has no recent history is likely to be getting the balance to close the account. If the customer is a valuable one, the CRM system should give prompts for making offers to keep the customer. The CRM system may show that a calling customer has a Certificate of Deposit that expires next week. Do they want to roll it over? A customer may have an momentous birthday, like thirty or forty, next week. Isn't that a good time to begin a retirement savings account? So the CRM system provides a lot of actionable data, but it must be used. People must take initiative even if selling is not part of their function. Cross-functional incentives must be put in place to encourage the initiative. Functional leaders need to buy into the coordination of customer touch points across all functions. The organization must be designed to facilitate e-coordination.

The leader as organization designer can choose any or all of the methods described to foster the use of voluntary and e-coordination processes. The leader needs to become skilled at these methods, because more and more coordination processes are taking place at the grassroots level on a voluntary basis. The increasing availability of new information technology will continue the trend, as more decisions continue to be made at the point of customer contact by cross-functional groups.

As mentioned earlier in this chapter, a key goal of the organization designer is to match the coordination needs of the business's strategy with the appropriate types and amount of lateral processes. To implement simple business strategies, a functional structure and voluntary processes may be sufficient. But for many companies today, more coordination is needed to address all the dimensions of the strategy. Formal groups and integrators may then be the solution. These are discussed in the next chapter.

5

Creating and Integrating Group Processes

The decision to augment voluntary and e-coordination lateral processes with formal processes—either formal groups or formal groups plus integrators—will make the leader more of a decision shaper. The voluntary processes described in Chapter Four arise spontaneously; they are a form of organization from the bottom up. With the formal lateral processes, the leader is more directly involved in the creation, the staffing, and the goal setting. Thus there is more organization from the top down.

There are several reasons for a more active role by the leader in the design of the lateral processes. If an issue arises and no voluntary process forms in response, management must create a group to deal with the issue. Management—from its perspective—may, in fact, become aware of an issue before it even appears to be an issue at the lower levels of the organization. Or management may want to augment or modify a voluntary process already in existence.

From a more global perspective, management shapes a lateral process to make it more compatible with other efforts, with resources, and with the overall strategy. For example, at the grassroots level an issue may be seen as a sales and marketing problem, while from management's viewpoint the issue may be larger, involving operations as well. Thus management may want to increase or change membership in a cross-functional team. It may add a person who would profit from the experience or an experienced person who could commit more resources.

Finally, management must set priorities about the types and amount of lateral processes it wishes to undertake. With limited resources, a company cannot simultaneously undertake product, customer, process, vendor, and twenty-five improvement teams at the same level of the organization. Management must set priorities about where talent needs to be invested. The priorities should set the strategic direction and focus the organization.

Formal Groups

Formal groups augment the efforts of voluntary processes. When there is a need for more decision making, a team, task force, or council is created to focus on a set of issues. However, rather than being a substitute for voluntary processes, formal groups are used in addition to them and, indeed, build on the same capabilities. There is currently a great deal of writing about using teams (Cohen, 1993; Smith and Katzenbach, 1992) and about team building (Dyer, 1988). These topics will not be repeated here. But there are some important design issues.

Design of Formal Groups

All groups, no matter what type, are subject to the same design choices. These are summarized as follows:

Bases. The bases for lateral processes are the same as the bases for structure, that is, function, product, market, geography, and work flow. If one is chosen for the structure, the other four are candidates for lateral processes. Each candidate has the same positives and negatives as the structural type. Just as strategy drives the choice of structure, it should help set the priorities here. The organization designer should also decide how much time and effort should be devoted to each.

Charter. The scope, mission, and authority of the groups must be defined. What issues are to be addressed? What resource levels can the group commit? Management should define the groups' charters so that they are compatible with the charter of the hierarchical structure and supplement it. In addition, management should look for overlapping efforts between various groups and define conflict resolution processes.

Staffing. The people who participate in a group are central to its efficient functioning. A representative should be chosen from each affected unit. All should have a position within their unit that gives them access to the information relevant to the issues that will be addressed and the authority to commit their unit. If the group is to be a unit making decisions in reasonable time frames, members must possess both information and authority. The roles created by mirror image structures are ideal for this purpose.

The mirror image structure also creates roles in which the manager's job in the vertical hierarchy is consistent with the job in the lateral processes. A less than ideal situation is when the managers of a company are spread across thirty to thirty-five teams. Each manager has four or five team assignments in addition to a full-time job. Very little will be accomplished in these teams. Organization designers should strive to staff groups so that managers are given only one cross-functional team assignment. Further, the team assignment should have as much overlap as possible with the full-time job.

Conflict. Conflict management is a required skill in an ever-changing world. The group needs a way to manage the inevitable differences in points of view constructively. Individual members need group problem-solving and conflict management skills. The purpose is to use different points of view to stimulate information exchange and learning. Although each member will see a portion of a situation, the group problem solving will afford a total view.

Rewards. Participants will have little energy with which to confront conflict and solve problems if they perceive little reward resulting from their efforts (Lawler, 1990). The person's team performance should count as much as the line job performance in evaluations. The team performance component can be gauged from the meeting of team goals, such as cycle time. Additional input can come from evaluations of other team members or of the team leader.

Leader Role. There is an emerging view that teams may not need a formal leader. And indeed, for groups with a reasonable number of members and some self-management experience, a designated leader may not be required. Instead, a different leader will emerge depending on the issue at hand and those in the group most capable to handle it. Most organizations, however, designate a leader to plan agendas, convene the group, lead discussions, and communicate the group's decisions.

Rather than creating a full-time integrator role, a leader may be chosen from the function most affected by the group task or from a dominant function. Boeing design-and-build teams are led by design engineers; Procter & Gamble brand teams are led by advertising brand managers. In both cases, the natural work closely resembles that of the leadership task.

Another option is a rotating leader. The leader changes as the function most affected changes with each successive stage of the group's work. For example, Dow-Corning rotates the leadership of new product teams. Initially the leader comes from R&D, then from manufacturing, and eventually from marketing as the product nears distribution. Over the product development cycle, the group gets a general management leader, but gets it through sequential handoffs from one function to another.

Simple Group Structures

The design of lateral group structures can vary from simple ones that have only a few cross-functional product teams to complex multidimensional and multilevel structures. The coordination needs of the strategy will dictate how complex a form is necessary.

The use of simple teams has been a management strategy for some time, since the aerospace companies began using cross-functional teams in the 1960s. Today, companies are focusing on work flows and creating cross-functional work flow teams to gain speed and reengineer processes.

In all simple structures, the designer tries to create an end-to-end task, so that the team has a complete piece of work. In this manner, the team controls most of the factors that influence its performance outcomes. The team can then be independently measured on its performance and held accountable for it. Management can give considerable decision-making power to such a group.

In the electronics industry, new products are introduced annually and last only eighteen months. Companies use cross-functional teams dedicated to the product for the entire eighteen months. The team develops the product, introduces it, manages it, and takes it off the market; the more complete the task, the more control the team has. It is thus easier for the team to generate a plan and for management to delegate decision making to it. The team is measured on total profitability over the product's life cycle, making it easier to reward the members for the team's performance.

Complex Group Structures

Teams can become complex for three reasons. The first is the complexity of the task being managed. The auto industry uses cross-functional teams to design new products called *platforms*. There is a platform team that consists of all the leaders of the design groups designing the platform. But the platform is further broken into its components—chassis, power train and engine, interior, exterior body, and so on. Each component has a cross-functional team designing that component to become part of the overall platform. So there is an overarching platform team managing the subteams for all the components. For large, complicated products like autos, large computers, aircraft, and the like, the team structure will reflect the architecture of the product itself. The team structure will become a hierarchy of cross-functional teams.

A second reason for complexes of teams and subteams is the number of people participating on the teams. When fifty to seventy-five people are involved in designing a component for an automobile, the team is usually split into a core team and extended team to include all the other participants. In the 1980s, the engineers designed the car and passed the design to manufacturing. Today, the auto companies use simultaneous engineering. They follow initiatives with titles like "Design and Manufacturability," "Design for Quality," "Design for Serviceability," and so on. These initiatives mean that people from manufacturing, quality, service, marketing, sales, and even customers are part of the design process. These initiatives create very large cross-functional teams.

Teams also become complex when the business has multiple dimensions. Although the Boeing 777 design-and-build teams are created around sections of the product, Boeing also forms customer teams for customers like United Airlines or All Nippon Airways. The difficulty arises because the design-and-build teams want every plane to be the same so as to reduce costs and cycle time while the customer teams want the planes to be different for each customer. Hence, there is a need for dialogue and conflict resolution. Complex structures become necessary when teams are interdependent and possibly in conflict. With complex team structures, the organization designer must solve two problems. First, the designer must create processes to coordinate and communicate across teams. Second, the designer must create a process to resolve interteam conflicts. An example will serve to illustrate these concepts.

Multidimensional Team. A personal computer business is organized by function and uses cross-functional product teams for notebook computers, laptops, low-end personal computers, high-performance personal computers, and so on. The product teams manage the product variety and reduce the time to market for new products. New products, which used to take two to three years to develop, are now created in one year, and last about eighteen months. Speed is one of the bases of competition.

This business has also become cost-driven, and many components are contracted out to low-cost producers. But component costs are volume-driven. Thus, if each product team chooses the same component and the same vendor, the volume from the business can be concentrated on a single vendor, and lower costs obtained. To agree on a common component and vendor for each component on each product, the company created component teams for keyboards, cathode ray tubes, printed circuit boards, flat panel displays, and several other potential common components.

The issue to be managed in this example is the potential conflict between the component teams and the product teams. Conflicts can surface in two ways. First, the product design engineers usually prefer components that optimize the performance of their product. But common components mean that a component will fit all products and optimize none of them. So the design engineers may fight the idea of using common components at all or they may disagree about which component should be the common one. The other point of conflict may involve the attempt to reach consensus across the product and component teams; this process can constrain the speed of the product design team. Top speed is attained when each team makes design decisions independently. The design of the team structure and the guidance from top management are the keys to achieving common components and speedy launch of new products simultaneously.

Top management of the computer company has articulated a strategy that places cost as the primary criterion for resolving conflicts. The strategy shifts the burden of proof to the engineers to show how a unique component will result in a substantial price and performance difference. Management also challenges the engineers to achieve high performance while using standard, common components. Top management's strategy is to provide criteria for decentralizing decisions to product and component

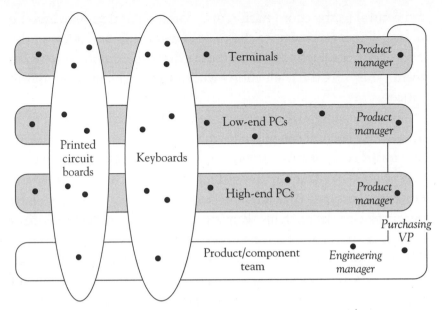

FIGURE 5.1. Product and Component Team Combination.

teams. The same criteria serve the dispute settlement process across the teams.

The organization design of the product teams and component teams is shown in Figure 5.1. Each product team is a cross-functional unit led by a product manager from engineering. Engineering and purchasing representatives working on printed circuit boards and keyboards are members of both the product teams and the component teams. They serve as the links between the two teams. They are joined on the component teams by their counterparts working on other product teams. Component teams are chaired by technically trained managers from purchasing. In turn, the component team leaders, product team leaders, and product managers all form a conflict resolution team chaired by the purchasing vice president. A manager from engineering, usually a computer architect, participates as well.

The key features of the design are the linkages. The engineering and purchasing representatives who participate on both teams are central to the coordination and communication between the teams. The other links are the people who serve as leaders of the two teams. Collectively, they constitute the conflict resolution team. They link the team efforts with a thorough but rapid appeal process.

In this example, the teams permit a functional organization to focus simultaneously on products and on component vendors. With purchased components accounting for 70 percent to 80 percent of cost of goods sold, and with product speed and cost central to the customer purchase decision, the business chooses to manage new products with the complex team structure. Each product requires a general manager and each component requires a general manager. The intention is to rapidly generate a family of new, low-cost products. The speed of the product teams is constrained by the use of common components. But the more effective the participants are at communicating, sharing databases, and resolving conflicts, the faster they can generate new and low-cost products. The ability to execute a multidimensional decision process becomes a competitive advantage in the marketplace.

A Spectrum of Design. Thus the organization design of teams can vary from simple to complex. The easiest design to manage is a series of simple teams, each with end-to-end responsibility for its task. Because each team controls its own destiny, the most freedom can be granted and the best speed in execution obtained. The teams get more complicated when the number of participants becomes too large for a single team to execute end-to-end responsibility. Teams are also more complicated when a business wants to be responsive with products but must simultaneously respond to vendors and customers. Size of group and multidimensional responsiveness both lead to the design of linkages across groups and a hierarchical conflict-resolution process. The ability to execute multidimensional team processes rapidly enhances responsiveness and achieves a competitive advantage.

E-Coordination of Teams

One of the factors that is permitting larger and more complex teams to work together is the placement of the New Product Development (NPD) process on the Web. The auto industry has always automated the NPD process by using systems for Computer Aided Design (CAD), Computer Aided Manufacturing (CAM), and Computer Aided Engineering (CAE). These separate systems are being migrated to the Web, integrated, and extended to include suppliers. When connected, the new system will permit cross-functional teams to view a component or a whole car on their screens and communicate by voice. Each participant could suggest changes that can be seen by the whole team. These three-dimensional systems will also contain analysis packages to compute the cost, weight, and space implications. With a digital design, the car can be simulated for noise, vibration, and harshness. It can be tested on a virtual track.

One version is DaimlerChrysler's Fast Car Program (Hall, 2000, p. 193). The program links design, manufacturing, engineering, quality, finance, purchasing, sales, and marketing into a seamless system. All decisions can be viewed and evaluated simultaneously by all functions on the team. When Fast Car is completed there will be four thousand internal users and five thousand external users among suppliers and large customers. All will have access to a "3D Homepage" and all the data behind it. The platform team can see the whole project and see the consequences of a decision simultaneously. It will take time and cost out of the NPD process.

Success will still depend on teamwork. This integrated system will need to be matched with an integrated organization capable of e-coordination.

In the examples discussed thus far, team leaders were put in place without much explanation of the integrating role. The next section discusses the design decisions involved in choosing the type of integrator and integrating roles. These roles are adopted when the teams need a full-time—and often neutral—leader. The teams will require leaders when coordination is challenging, the performance targets are difficult, and the team efforts are high priority.

Integrating Roles

The most complex aspect of the lateral process is the creation of full-time leaders. Integrating roles create the truly multidimensional organization. There is a need for these roles when a company wants to attain functional excellence, generate new products and services, and be responsive to customers. Such capacity is a requirement for some businesses in a complex, changing world.

The flexibility to deal with customers, vendors, and processes comes at a cost. First, there is the obvious investment in salaries for people who are to coordinate the work of others rather than produce work of their own. The investment, however, should yield faster time to market or better customer knowledge and relationships. The second cost is the time spent resolving conflicts. Managers for customer segments, products, and functions all see the world differently. Disagreement and the inability to resolve it effectively can slow the company responses and turn the focus inward rather than on customers.

In contrast, the ability to deal with controversy and different views increases the company's ability to respond to a variety of opportunities and threats. This ability is a competitive advantage.

Design of Integrating Roles

The organization design issues for integrating roles revolve around the power base from which the integrator will influence decisions. Managers in the hierarchical structure have authority and control of resources, but what is the power base of the integrator? How much power and influence does the integrator need? The power base of the integrator will be shaped by the following factors:

- Structure of the role
- Staffing choice
- Status of the role
- Information systems
- Planning processes
- Reward systems
- Budget authority
- Dual authority

Structure of the Role. The ideal structure is to have the integrator report directly to the general manager. The three usual practices are shown in Figure 5.2. Because there are usually several product lines, product managers report to a product management function, as shown in version A of the figure. The product management function may have some additional people working on costs and schedules of product programs.

In a variation of this practice, the product managers report to the R&D or engineering manager. Version B shows this method in high-technology industries. Version C shows another variation, seen in consumer packaged goods industries, where products and brands have long life cycles. Both versions B and C place the product manager in a function that is dominant for the industry. The variation in version A shows a more powerful, more neutral, and more general manager–like structure, because it is not associated with any function and has direct access to the general manager. The variations are appropriate for businesses that are technology-driven (version B) or market-driven (version C). Other variations are also possible (Galbraith, 1994, chap. 5).

Staffing Choice. The people who play the integrator roles are the key factors in implementing the multidimensional organization. Few people who can play the general management role also have the skills to influence without authority. The key is to select people

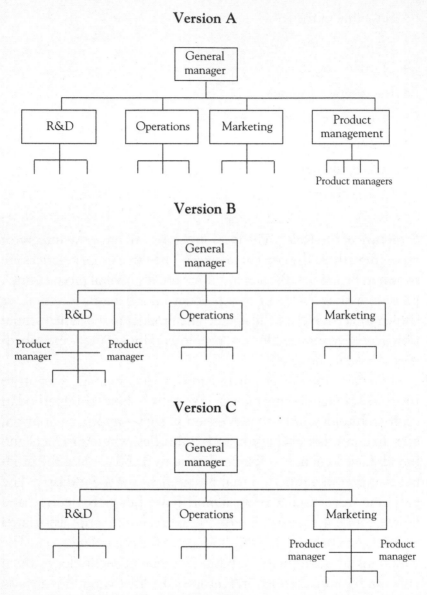

FIGURE 5.2. Product Manager Variations.

who have the interpersonal and networking skills to be personally persuasive. Technical skills are desirable but secondary.

The best way to find these individuals is to grow them. If people experience rotational assignments early in their careers, create their own personal networks, participate in lateral groups, and then chair a lateral group, they are usually ready to play a process integrator or project manager role. This process creates the generalist skills, builds the person's network, and teaches influence skills early on. Management's role is to select the successful participants in the company's lateral processes because these people become the best integrators.

Status of the Role. There is a better likelihood that integrators will be able to influence if the role has status. What constitutes status varies with the culture of the company. Usually, status can be enhanced by increasing the rank of the integrating role or by locating the office of the integrator on the executive floor. Alternatively, the status of the role can be enhanced by staffing it with senior people with good track records. Whatever type of status-enhancer is used, its purpose is to increase the ability of the integrator to exercise influence, even if the role has no authority.

Information Systems. Multidimensional organizations require multidimensional information. It is a real advantage to have the capacity to convert data into information on revenues, costs, and profits by customer, product, geography, and function. This information arms the integrators with facts and knowledge they can use to influence others. The integrators can also contract with the line organization and then monitor the contractual agreements. Such rich data gives the integrator a cross-company visibility into a product, customer, or process that no one else has. The visibility and facts give the integrator substantial influence.

In contrast, a lack of integrated information systems presents a large impediment to companywide integration. Many reengineering projects to move processes to the Web attempt to obtain visibility across units and build databases so everyone works from the same information.

Planning Processes. The multidimensional information system can be used to support a multidimensional planning process. When

	Sales	Marketing	Information technology	Install and repair	Network operations
Health Services					
Financial services					
Governments					
Distribution					
Manufacturing					
Other					

EXHIBIT 5.1. Planning Matrix.

based on valid data, the planning process can become the arena for focusing the natural contentions of the different perspectives for resolution. An example will illustrate this point.

A former Bell company has created market segment business units. The planning matrix for the business unit serving medium-size companies is shown in Exhibit 5.1. The functional organizations are listed across the top. The market segments managed by integrators are listed down the left side. The planning process amounts to a series of discussions between segment managers and functional managers. The managers must agree on revenues, costs, and investments in each of the rows and columns; there are always more requests for resources than resources available. The business unit general manager sets initial guidelines, facilitates resolution of crucial disputes, and manages the entire process by convening all participants. When it is completed, the planning matrix allows all managers to shoot for the same targets.

This planning process requires information to support it. It needs participants skilled at problem solving in conflict situations. Finally, it requires a general manager skilled at managing the process and comfortable with managing conflict.

Reward Systems. The step from the planning process to the reward system is a natural one. The managers on either side of the planning matrix have agreed on their goals. It is important for all the managers to make the goals in all of their individual cells in the

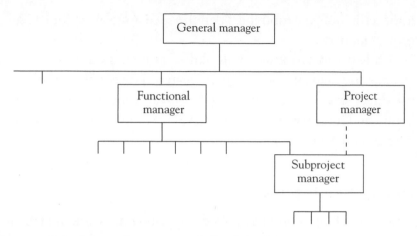

FIGURE 5.3. Matrix Structure with Dual Authority.

Source: Galbraith, J., *Competing with Flexible Lateral Organizations, 2/E,* ©1994. Reprinted/adapted by permission of Pearson Education, Inc., Upper Saddle River, New Jersey.

matrix, not just in the total of all the cells (traditionally the normal practice). Then the managers become jointly accountable and are responsible for the same goals. The information system, planning process, and reward system form an integrated package of management practices that support the multidimensional organization.

Budget Authority. Another way to enhance the integrator's role is to give it control over the budget for its product, process, or market. The organization designer specifies which budget categories and amounts are involved in order to enhance the integrator's execution of the coordination task.

Dual Authority. The final step in creating a power base for the integrator is to give that person authority over the people in the function. This step creates a matrix structure that contains two reporting lines. Usually one person is selected as a subproject manager, as shown in Figure 5.3.

The subproject manager alone works for two bosses. The dual authority is implemented by having both bosses participate in the joint setting of goals and joint performance assessment for the sub-project manager.

Only organizations that are skilled at lateral processes should attempt the dual authority step. It creates a power balance between the dimensions of the structure—but it can generate its own set of conflicts. The situation can easily produce more disagreements and confusion than flexibility.

Putting It All Together

The formal lateral processes of groups, integrators, and matrix are powerful methods to use when management must take a strong role in the lateral organization. Through these processes a multidimensional organization is created, intended to increase the company's flexibility in responding to vendors, markets, technologies, governments, and so on. The organization is more likely to be capable of extensive communication and cooperation, as well as rapid escalation and resolution of conflicts. The next chapters present some additional examples of combinations of structures and lateral processes. First is a multidimensional structure showing how companies can configure themselves to respond to many differing pressures at the same time. Next are examples of companies organizing around the increasingly important dimension of the customer.

6

Designing a Reconfigurable Organization

Every company needs an organization that changes as quickly as its business changes. If not, the company is falling behind. To keep from falling behind, many companies are devoting enormous amounts of time and energy to change management. This task can be made less difficult and less time consuming if some effort is focused on designing organizations from the outset to be more easily changeable. If change is constant, why not design our organizations to be constantly and quickly changeable? It is this easily changeable or reconfigurable organization that is the subject of this chapter.

Competing with No Sustainable Advantage

Organizations have always been created to execute business strategies. As mentioned in Chapter Two, different strategies have led to different organizations. But when advantages do not last long, neither do the organizations that execute them. In the past, management crafted a winning business formula and erected barriers to entry to sustain the advantage. Then management created an organization structure around functions, products or services, markets, or geographies that was designed to deliver the success formula. To complete the integrity of the organization, planning and budgeting processes, information systems, new product development

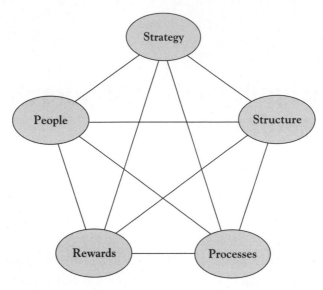

FIGURE 6.1. The Star Model.

processes, compensation systems, selection and promotion criteria, career paths, performance appraisals, and training and development sequences would all be designed and aligned with each other and with the organization's strategy and structure. Such an aligned organization would execute the strategy with as little friction as possible. This thinking resulted in concepts like the star model described in Chapter Two, which is repeated for your convenience as Figure 6.1.

Today, in many industries, that model of organization design is flawed. The success formulas it generates do not last very long (D'Aveni, 1994). The advantages around which the organization is designed are quickly copied or even surpassed by high-speed competitors. Every advantage is temporary. Therefore, to focus and align the organization is to become vulnerable. As a result, some people have concluded that alignment is no longer a useful organizational design criterion. I agree that alignment around a focused strategy can impede change to a new strategy, but it is the continued focus on a nonsustainable advantage that is the flaw, rather than the alignment itself. The point can be made by focusing on the alternative—misalignment. Misalignment of strategy, structure, and processes will cause activities to conflict, units to work at cross-purposes, and organizational energy to dissipate over many frictions. Instead, we need a new, aligned organizational design. We need to have organization structures and processes that are easily reconfigured and realigned with a constantly changing strategy.

Thus the challenge is to design organizations to execute strategies when there are no sustainable competitive advantages. When product advantages are not sustainable over time, the winners will be those who create a *series* of short-term temporary advantages. Under this scenario, the leaders will be future-oriented and will continuously create capabilities that lead to customer value. They will move quickly to combine these capabilities to match and surpass current advantages (including their own). They will outmaneuver competitors by stringing together a series of moves and countermoves, as in a game of chess. Those companies with the capabilities for flexible response and a variety of moves over the course of time will most likely win. The reconfigurable organization is the means to execute this continuous strategy shifting.

The Reconfigurable Organization

The reconfigurable organization results from the skilled use of three capabilities. First, the organization is reconfigured by forming teams and networks across organizational departments. These lateral structures require an extensive internal networking capability as described in Chapters Four and Five. Second, the organization uses internal prices, markets, and marketlike devices to coordinate the complexity of multiple teams. And finally, the organization forms partnerships to secure capabilities that it does not have. These partnerships require an external networking capability, as discussed in Chapter Nine. The three capabilities are best illustrated with an example.

The example company is a manufacturer of consumer baking products—cookies and crackers and so on. The firm had competencies in brand management and distribution. It had a network of bakeries across North America and a logistics system that could deliver directly from the bakery to the retail store. Baking has always been a just-in-time business. This company's brands and its distribution system (only Coca-Cola and Pepsi could match it) had been its advantages and its barriers to entry.

In the 1980s these advantages came under attack. Retailers and their private label suppliers could easily match the company's product quality at significantly lower prices. Also, the baker's products were high fat and high calorie. Hence, the company's products were being avoided by both the budget conscious and the health conscious.

The company's resurgence began with its discovery of a low-fat ingredient that maintained the product's taste. After the U.S. Food and Drug Administration approved use of this ingredient, the company began reformulating its most popular brands and focused promotions on the health segment. The new products literally flew off of the shelves. The reformulation revived the brands and created an advantage that the private labels could not match.

To capitalize further on the product popularity, the company expanded into all possible distribution channels. However, different channels require different packaging. The company then created partnerships with independent manufacturers (called *co-packers*) to provide multiple packages. It now provides products in enormous boxes for the discount club stores and single-serving portions for vending machines and convenience stores.

Next, the company took the new ingredient into new categories such as breakfast products and snacks where it could create an advantage. It created new products for these new categories with partners and co-packers because the products (like granola bars) were not baked. The expansion provided a new business in different aisles of the grocery store. The new products could also be kept fresh by using the company's existing delivery system. Other manufacturers of breakfast foods did not have this capability nor the low-fat ingredient.

The company also created partnerships (which it called *category management*) with two of its larger customers. These customers turned the management of the entire cookie and cracker aisle over to the baking company. The baking company's skills in brand management, sophisticated analysis of bar code data, and knowledge of the cookie and cracker category allowed both customer and manufacturer to increase their respective profitabilities. By coordinating the product and cash flow from bakery to store, the partners could minimize working capital. The grocery customers are now interested in packaging that is unique to them. Here again, the baking company, with its packaging flexibility through its external network of partnerships, is able to meet its customers' needs.

In summary, our example company created an advantage through its discovery of a low-fat ingredient which maintains the product taste. Using its existing capabilities in logistics and brand management, it successfully targeted and dominated the health segment. It created a multichannel, multipackage capability to enlarge the population that its products can reach. It used the ingredient and its logistics to enter a new category (breakfast foods). The ingredient advantage will buy time for the company while it builds knowledge in the new category. And finally, its enhanced reputation, brand management, logistics, and flexible packaging capabilities made it an attractive partner for large retailers. The company has created a *series* of advantages by combining and recombining new capabilities and old ones to address new products, new segments, new channels, and new customer relationships. It is a good example of the continuous creation of advantages. The baking company creates and implements an initiative which gives it advantage. Then it quickly moves on to the next advantage. What is next?

The company's next steps are also instructive. Its managers focused their attention on the search for another new ingredient, one with low fat, low calories, and good taste. But when no ingredient was found, no new advantages were introduced. As a result the competition not only caught up but launched an initiative of its own. A competitor focused on the old product lines, added some flavor enhancers, and addressed itself to the children's segment. This segment valued flavor and, unfortunately, was less health conscious. The competitor stole market share in the category as a result.

The share loss was a wake-up call to the company. It retaliated with its own flavor enhancers and followed with a marketing initiative focused on kids. It continued to develop its segment capabilities of working across products and brands, and focusing them on new segments. The next segment was Hispanics. This segment continues to grow in numbers and in disposable income. The bakery focused on a dozen products and the six major Hispanic markets like the Mexican Southern California and the Cuban South Florida. The segment lined up co-packers for packaging in the Spanish language and prepared ads for the Spanish-speaking media.

The company also returned to the expansion of its existing initiatives. It expanded its partners in category management from two to five, with more being pursued. It entered the snack category with a partner. It avoided Frito-Lay and positioned itself against the number three and four players in the market. The company also positioned itself as healthier because its products were baked rather than fried.

Any finally, the bakery has found a way to profit from its distribution capability. The company has become a leader in collaborative logistics. That is, using the Web as a central coordination tool, producers, retailers, and truckers can share trucks and warehouses when going to and from the same locations. It has joined ten other manufacturers and its category management partners in a new venture in collaborative logistics. The venture has been a major source of savings and new revenue.

So the company appears to be back on track. It is continuing to create new sources of advantage from combining its new and old capabilities. It also knows that if it rests and does not generate the next sources of advantage, someone else will. As a result, it still searches for new ingredients. But it also searches for new categories, new customers, new channels, new segments, and so on. It has become a player in the era of temporary advantages.

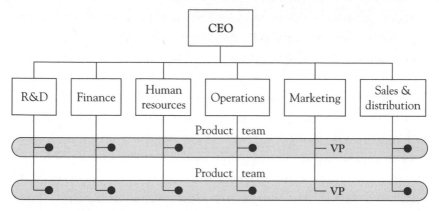

FIGURE 6.2. Product Team Organization.

Creating Reconfigurability

This strategy of creating a series of short-term advantages can only be effective if the company has an organization that can execute it. Prior to the discovery of the low-fat ingredient, the company was organized functionally around research and development, operations, marketing, sales and distribution, finance, and human resources. Like most packaged consumer goods companies, it used cross-functional product line teams. These teams, shown in Figure 6.2, are chaired by the product vice presidents from marketing. It had reasonably good cross-functional relationships. Quite a few of the top management group had cross-functional experience. In addition, for about five years, the company was encouraging project management experience. Almost all managers had attended the project management course. Almost all had worked on cross-functional project teams. The company built on this base to implement the continuous strategy shifts.

The first organizational change was the creation of a third team that was focused on the health segment and was to reformulate and relaunch the company's products. This team was chaired by a full-time marketing vice president. As with the two existing teams, each function contributed a representative who had the time (at least 50 percent), the authority to represent the function, and the information about the function to be used in problem solving. The main difference was that the segment team was both cross-function and cross-product.

The new category was addressed by another cross-functional unit chaired by a vice president from marketing. But this team was full-time and dedicated to the effort of breaking into a new category. Several dedicated salespeople worked for the unit and created the new sales approach for the new category. This team reported directly to the CEO to get the attention and focus that a new business requires. The reporting relationship also gave it leverage with its partner.

A similar team was created for the new channels. A vice president from marketing chaired the team but reported to the senior vice president for sales and distribution. All functions, except research and development, contributed a full-time, dedicated manager. There was no research and development representation because there were no new products involved. The channel team bought products from the factories and managed the relationships with co-packers who packaged the products.

Following these changes, two more dedicated cross-functional units were formed for the two customer partnerships. These units also consisted of full-time, dedicated people from all functions, again except research and development. The units were chaired by the account manager for the customer and reported to the senior vice president of sales and distribution. Both the channel and customer teams were cross-function and cross-product units. This new organization is shown in Figure 6.3.

In the meantime, the finance function was redesigning the accounting system. It implemented an activity-based cost system. At the same time, it installed enterprise software to automate the new system. The result is that profit and loss measurement can be applied to all of the strategic initiatives. The products, segments, categories, channels, and customers are all profit-and-loss measurable. The human resources department is redesigning the reward

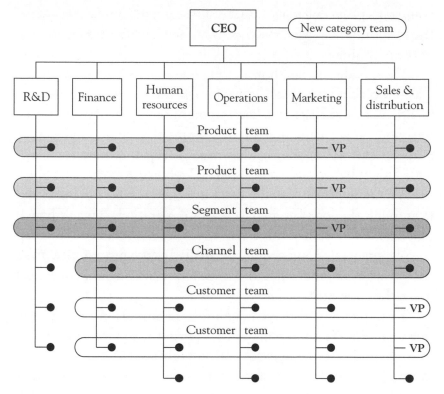

FIGURE 6.3. Multidimensional Organization.

systems to incorporate team-based rewards. Each of these teams is in fact a miniature business unit.

In this way, the example company has configured and reconfigured itself from a functional structure with brand managers to a multistructure based on functions, products, segments, categories, channels, and customers. It is a multiple profit and loss structure that can be flexibly changed to any dimension that will support the next strategic advantage. The company is creating the capability to organize any way it wants to organize. So instead of choosing to organize by function *or* product *or* market segment to implement a sustainable brand advantage, the company is organized by function *and* product *and* segment *and* channel *and* customer to implement a series of constantly changing, short-term advantages. After the company's pause due to its unsuccessful search for a new ingredient, the new initiatives were matched with new organizational units to implement them.

These additions are shown in Figure 6.4. A segment group was added, which is an umbrella group for the three current segments—health, kids, and Hispanics. Each segment has its own team. A similar group was created for the five teams that serve as customer partners in the category management service. A new team was added for collaborative logistics. A VP reporting to the sales function chairs the team. On the team are the distribution managers from sales, the logistics managers from operations, and a finance manager. Even though this is a new venture, it still needs to keep the plants supplied and customers satisfied as the first priority. Thus the creation of groups like the ones for segments and customers make the structure scalable.

To implement this reconfigurable organization, a company needs an aligned set of policies that permit it to form and reform internal and external networks of capabilities. Let me describe in more detail the elements of the star model that support the capability to reconfigure.

Structure

The structure of the reconfigurable organization consists of a stable part and a changing part. The changing part was described in the course of the example as the company configured miniature businesses around products, segments, channels, and customers. This changing part is the reconfigurable part, which changes with changes in competitive strategy.

The functional structure is the stable part. This stable structure is both home and host to the company's employees. It is home to the specialists and experts in food science, distribution, manufacturing technologies, analysis of bar code data, and other competencies that the company has built. These people tend not to rotate across functions but do participate in the cross-functional teams.

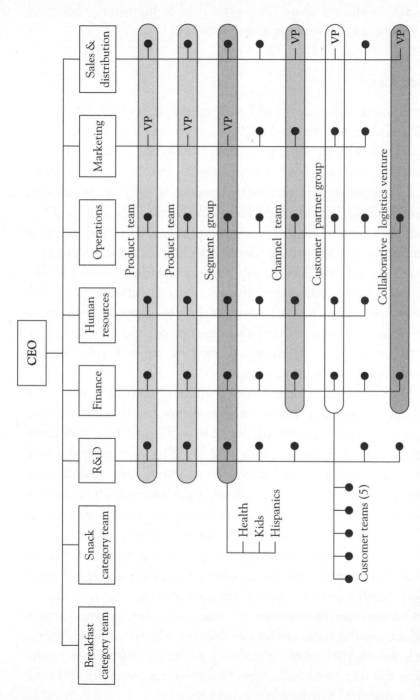

FIGURE 6.4. Fully Reconfigurable Organization.

The functional structure is also the host to managers who move across functions or rotational assignments.

Processes

The first area, information and goal-setting processes, is often overlooked and underestimated in its power to define an organization's capabilities. The reconfigurable organization needs accounting systems, data structures, and planning processes that allow it to operate as a collection of miniature business units. All the data must be available to all the parties. As mentioned earlier, the costs and revenues must be assignable to products, segments, channels, and so on so that profitability can be identified. Policies for transfer prices need to accurately reflect market prices to coordinate resource allocations between miniature business units themselves and with external partners. The complexity of coordinating all these miniature business units is aided by the use of prices and markets. Flexible, reconfigurable organizations must be aligned with flexible, reconfigurable accounting systems.

The management team must be skilled at the timely resolution of conflicts. Constant change brings constant conflict. For example, the products from the health segment stole sales from the traditional cookie and cracker product lines. What is best for the total company? There are frequent priority decisions when resources are shared. Which channel and customers get supplied when the new products are in short supply? At the bakery, there was the "Monday morning meeting" where these issues were thrashed out. Attendance varied from ten to eighteen people. The information systems and the problem-solving management teams are necessary for the timely decisions in a reconfigurable organization.

A second set of processes are the common processes for new product development, order fulfillment, and strategic planning. These are another source of stability. In the reconfigurable organization, the structure changes but the processes are stable and common across the miniature business units.

And next, there needs to be a strong management team. There is really only one business and one Profit and Loss statement that counts. That is the company P&L. However, the strategy shifting and reconfiguring of the organization requires that it be decomposed into many miniature business units. In this way, each unit can pursue different initiatives, but they impact both positively and negatively on the company P&L. The integration of all these units is the task of the management team, which must set priorities, allocate resources, and resolve the inevitable conflicts.

A joint project between the marketing and the finance functions has been launched to create modeling tools to help determine the profit impacts of initiatives in products, segments, channels, and so on. Marketing has the data-mining tools and the databases. Finance has the financial analysis skills. These are to be combined into modeling techniques and simulations to support the leadership in launching and evaluating the miniature business.

People

Equally important is the area of human resources. The HR policies must be aligned to create the behaviors and mind-sets that support reconfigurability. The conflicts within a unit and between units over priorities and transfer prices can sap the energy from a miniature business unit. The participants need to be cross-functionally skilled, have cross-unit interpersonal networks, identify with the company as a whole, and be part of a reconfigurable culture. The various human resource policies are central to creating these skills and networks, and the overall culture (see Lawler, 1994).

These human resource policies start with hiring practices that recruit and attract people who fit the organization, not just the job. Jobs will change and new skills will be learned. But individual personalities and company values and culture are much less likely to change. Hence a person-organization fit is key to the reconfigurable organization. Personality tests, work simulations, and very extensive interviews are characteristic of hiring the person to fit the organization. For the reconfigurable organization, fondness for working in teams, ability to solve problems and handle conflicts, and the desire and potential to learn new skills are some of the personality attributes that are sought. For example, the baking company in the example uses a cross-functional interviewing process. Potential brand managers are interviewed by current brand managers and also by research scientists, manufacturing representatives, and sales managers with cross-functional experience. The company does not want a hot-shot marketer whose sole interest is the fast track through brand management. The person must also be acceptable to R&D and manufacturing. The intensive interview process selects people who will be effective in cross-functional work. This process also sends a message that "cross-function is the way we work" and helps build the reconfigurable culture.

Assignments and careers are also cross-functional for many managers. For example, R&D people often follow a new product they are working on into manufacturing and then into sales and distribution. At each step they learn new functional skills. They also learn the new product development process as they move along it. But just as important are the relationships they build, which add to their interpersonal network. The assignment process develops the individual and simultaneously develops the organization's network. The process builds the social capital on which reconfigurability is based.

Training is continuous and targeted at cross-unit participants. Project management training, for example, is given to cross-functional teams prior to beginning new projects. Other subjects are delivered to cross-unit groups consisting of people working at key interfaces. The purpose is always to simultaneously build know-how and know-who. The reconfigurable organization sees every training event and especially social events as opportunities to build know-who. The events are investments in building the company's social capital.

Rewards

Finally, the reward system needs to be equally flexible and reconfigurable (see Ledford, 1995). Yet nothing turns a manager into a conservative faster than a recommendation to change the compensation system. Because of this conservatism, compensation systems are the greatest barriers to change and flexibility. At a time when pay plans need to be approximate, flexible, simple, and valid, they are instead precise, complex, quantitative, nonaligned, out of date, and rigid. It takes years to study a pay system, reevaluate the jobs, pilot the new plan, and introduce it unit by unit. Far more speed and flexibility are needed.

The new, nimble reward systems have far fewer grades or bands than their predecessors—three rather than the thirty pay grades of old. Salaries are based on a person's skills and not the person's job title. Today we pay the person, not the job. Jobs change too quickly. So do the people—but the more they learn the more they earn. Often, skill-based pay is given as a one-time bonus for learning because skills also come and go. Employees get fewer raises—annuity-style additions to their pay—and more one-time bonuses that reflect current efforts without generating an ongoing financial obligation for the company.

The appraisal process is also moving away from a boss's appraisal to a team-based appraisal or 360-degree feedback model. There is less ranking of all 220 engineers along a single dimension and less complexity in the performance rating scales. Some organizations have an *appraisal day*—an automated process that is done and completed in less than a day. It is done easily and quickly and can be repeated more often for quickly changing environments. So pay systems are becoming more flexible in using more bonus and less annuity, simpler scales and grades, pay for skills rather than jobs, and encouraging faster changes and more experimentation.

Collectively these people and reward practices build the cross-unit skills, cross-unit interpersonal networks, and ultimately a

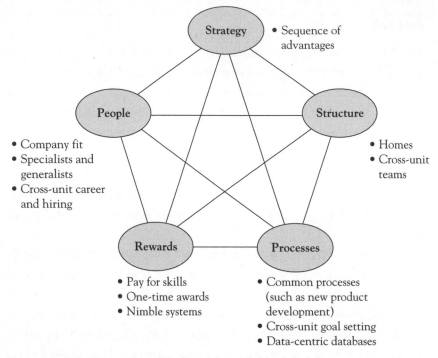

FIGURE 6.5. Reconfigurable but Aligned Star Model.

reconfigurable culture. Such practices build the skills and mind-sets to link functions, both inside and outside the company, into a miniature business unit. In this manner an organization is better positioned to capitalize on an opportunity and build a new capability. These capabilities can be combined and recombined in interesting ways to create the next advantage. But the lasting capability, and possibly a more sustainable source of advantage, is the capability of an organization to reconfigure itself. Figure 6.5 shows an aligned star model with the various practices that constitute the reconfigurable organization.

The Cost of Reconfigurability

Reconfigurability, unlike quality, is not free. It takes time and resources to build the information systems and human resource practices. A significant investment in recruiting and training is required. Then there is the investment of management in coordinating work within and between miniature business units. It is a communications-intense form of organization.

It is also fraught with the potential for problems. Companies may not always be able to find people who can manage conflict and who desire growth and development. Everyone is looking for team players. In addition, there is the potential for unresolved conflict. Transfer price issues can consume enormous amounts of time. As in matrix-type organizations, discussions in a reconfigurable organization can degenerate into endless internal negotiations that cut into the time available for customers. If not all policies are aligned, these internal frictions can absorb the company's energy. However, these costs and risks must be weighed against those of not being able to adjust to a reconfigurable competitor.

The reconfigurable organization is the companion to the continually shifting strategy. When competitive advantages do not last very long, neither do organizations. Instead, competitive advantage results from a string of short-term advantages delivered through a reconfigurable organization. The reconfigurable organization consists of a stable functional structure around which projects and miniature business units are continually formed, combined, and disbanded. These units can focus on products, channels, segments, customers, regions, suppliers, technologies, and so on. The company can literally and simultaneously organize any way it wants to organize. The reconfigurability rests on three capabilities:

- *Extensive internal cross-unit networking.* This capability is built through aligned human resource policies. It attracts, holds, and develops the flexible people who create the flexible organization.

- *Use of prices, markets, and marketlike devices to coordinate the multiple profit center units.* An accounting and information system that permits an accurate and flexible determination of profit and loss on any dimension is the central tool underlying this capability.

- *External networking with partners to expand the capabilities that can be combined in creating new advantages.* The same behavioral skills of cooperation, conflict management, and influence without authority that are used in internal networking are indispensable in managing external networks.

The final element is a top management team that sees its value added as designing and supporting the organization's reconfigurability.

7

Organizing Around the Customer

Chapter Six addressed issues of designing organizations around multiple dimensions. In this chapter the focus is on one dimension—the customer. Over the past decade companies have seen an increase in the strategic priority assigned to the customer dimension of the business. As a result many companies are organizing around the customer. Creating customer-facing organizational units is a challenge because these companies still have structures based on product lines, geography, and functions. This chapter addresses the challenge of creating and adding a customer dimension to the organization. The first section deals with the question, Why is the customer dimension increasing in importance? Then it asks, What capabilities will the company need to respond to the customer priority? It gives several examples of companies that have created customer-focused designs. The next chapter presents customer-focused structures. It also addresses another question, How do we build these new capabilities and integrate them with our existing capabilities?

The Rise of the Customer Dimension

The trend in most industries is toward the increasing importance of the customer. The factors causing this increase vary with the industry. Either individually or collectively, however, all businesses are experiencing the following changes in their environment:

- The globalization of customers
- The preference of customers for partnerships or relationships
- The customers' desire for solutions
- The rise of electronic commerce
- The steady increase in the power of the buyer

Globalization

Since 1985, the process of globalization has been driven by increasing amounts of foreign direct investment. The result is that more companies—and therefore more customers—have a direct presence in more countries. Often these global customers, who have a preferred customer status in their home countries and those where they are well established, object to receiving marginal treatment from a supplier's subsidiary upon entering a new country. These customers want a consistent and consistently high level of service in all countries where they buy from a supplier. Indeed one supplier had a customer point out that the supplier had thirty-seven sales forces coming to call with thirty-seven different standards of service and that was unacceptable. So the global customer is creating pressure on suppliers to coordinate across countries and businesses to provide better and more consistent service. This desire for cross-unit coordination can also be an advantage for the supplier. ABB was an early mover into many countries, and Eastern Europe in particular. It now uses its extensive presence to host and to provide services to its customers as they enter new countries where ABB is already present.

Customer Relationships

The pressure for coordination across existing structures is even greater when the customers want partnerships or relationships with their suppliers. Professional services firms are finding that clients want one or two global advertising agencies, auditors, cash management banking suppliers, and outsourcers for information technology. In most industries, customers are preferring fewer suppliers and establishing closer, longer-term relationships with them. For suppliers these global partnerships mean that the supplier must coordinate all countries in which the customer desires integrated services.

Solutions

Many customers are preferring solutions or systems instead of stand-alone products. To be sure, customers still order truckloads of desktop machines from computer manufacturers. However, they are also ordering trading rooms or call centers. At IBM, these solutions require the integration of multiple business units in multiple countries with multiple outside suppliers for the benefit of the customer. These solutions are not simply multiple stand-alone products bundled together and offered at a 10 percent discount. The customer-preferred solutions create value by packaging products and services in ways that the customers cannot easily do for themselves.

Solutions therefore require an in-depth knowledge of the customer and an ability to integrate product lines. The in-depth customer knowledge is needed to identify the solutions that will be seen as valuable by the customer. Then the supplier will need the ability to coordinate multiple profit centers from both inside and outside the company to create that value. Neither of these capabilities comes easily. Real estate agencies and banks have been searching for years for a mortgage solution for time-short homebuyers. Such a solution would combine the home loan, appraisal, title, title insurance, home insurance, and the other essentials into a single, sign-once package. Most of us are still waiting.

In addition to creating solutions, suppliers are also trying to customize them. Many companies are becoming sophisticated at identifying the most profitable customers. But when everyone pursues the most profitable customers, they compete away the profits. One approach to holding on to valuable customers is to customize the solutions that the customer wants. Customization requires yet more in-depth knowledge of the customer and additional capability to integrate products and services into unique solutions.

Electronic Commerce

Another integrating force pushing companies to focus on the customer is electronic commerce. When a company with a single brand uses its Web site as its storefront, it presents a single face to the customer. The Web site should be designed around the customers' needs and not around the supplier's product capabilities. The site should be designed to do business the way the customer wants to do business. To appear as a single entity to the customer, the company needs to integrate its businesses, subsidiaries, and functions and act like a single company.

The management of interactivity with customers is yet another integrating force. This topic was introduced in Chapter Five. Electronic connections with customers allow the company to recognize and remember each customer, to interact with them and remember more about them and then to customize the company's offerings based on the knowledge of the customer. Most companies, however, have not mastered integrated customer interactions. Interactivity requires the management of dialogues and content across all media with which the company interacts with the customer—Web site, e-mail, call center, salespersons, service representatives, and so on. The dialogue needs to be managed over time. The last contact with the customer needs to be remembered along with the last issue concerned and how it was resolved. The resolution needs to be recorded and then the next dialogue starts from there. All contacts and issues are to be remembered. The idea of interactivity is to collect and integrate all data across all functions, subsidiaries, and product lines so as to get a complete picture of each customer's value and needs. Only then can the company react as a single company and be seen by the customer as a single company.

Buyer Power

One of the main reasons that the factors mentioned thus far are taken seriously is that the power in the buyer-seller interaction has been moving to the buyer. In many industries global competition and industry overcapacity has given buyers more choice—and they are learning how to use it. Electronic commerce and information transparency have reduced seller knowledge advantages. So the competitive game has shifted to one of pleasing an increasingly more global, knowledgeable, and powerful customer.

One of the responses that companies have made is to increasingly organize around the customer. Whether it is global accounts, customer teams, or customer business units, the trend is to grow a customer dimension of the organization. The customer focus is a challenge in most companies, which are organized around product lines called business units, countries, and functions.

Deliver the Company to the Customer

To manage the evolving customer dimension most companies are organizing around the customer. This organization requires three capabilities that are intended to deliver the company to the customer. To be effective in organizing around the customer the company must take the following steps:

1. Create a customer-centric capability.
2. Perfect a lateral coordination capability (as described in Chapters Four and Five).
3. Create a leadership mind-set that says, "You compete with your organization."

Customer-Centric Capability

To create and customize solutions and appear as one company on a customer-friendly Web site, the company needs a customer-centric capability. This capability is often presented as a contrast to the product-centric capability. The Product-Centric column of Table 7.1 shows the management mind-set, culture, and star model organizational features of a company that takes this approach.

A product-centric company is one that tries to find as many uses and customers as possible for its product. Sony and its Walkman are typical of such a company and product. Until recently business units at Sony were even called Product Companies. As shown in the table, the profit centers, processes, measures, and human resource policies are all focused on creating great products. Taken together these policies create a culture of product excellence. Many good companies have thrived under this business model—Hewlett-Packard, P&G, and Chase Manhattan Consumer Bank, to name just a few. There is nothing wrong with this model when the customer wants to choose the best products and integrate them into a do-it-yourself solution. But when customers want ready-made solutions and a customer-friendly Web site, a company needs customer-centric capability as well as good products. The Customer-Centric column of Table 7.1 illustrates the change in approach.

A customer-centric company tries to find as many products as possible for each customer. It is based on economies of scope and on turning scope into solutions valuable to the customer. The customer-centric company becomes an expert in the customer's business. It helps the customer become more effective or more competitive. And perhaps the most telling feature of a customer-centric company, it is on the side of the buyer in the buyer-seller exchange. To stay on the customer's side, for example, Amazon.com does not accept advertising from sellers. On its new e-services Web site, the United Bank of Switzerland will offer competitive products, even those of Credit Swiss. Thus a customer-centric company will recommend the best product for a customer, even a competitor's product, so as to earn the trust of the customer. The customer-centric company then sees these customer relationships as assets to be managed. The business model of Amazon.com and AOL has evolved to the point where they are now selling access to their customer base. To appear on Amazon's Web site, a vendor must qualify, then pay a

TABLE 7.1. How Changing the Mind-Set Changes the Company.

	Product-Centric Company	Customer-Centric Company
Goal	Best product for customer	Best solution for customer
Value creation route	Cutting-edge products, useful features, new applications	Customizing for best total solution
Mental process	Divergent thinking: *How many possible uses of this product?*	Convergent thinking: *What combination of products is best for this customer?*
Organizational concept	Product profit centers, product reviews, product teams	Customer segments, customer teams, customer P&Ls
Most important process	New product development	Customer relationship management
Measures	• Number of new products • Percentage of revenue from products less than two years old • Market share	• Customer share of most valuable customers • Customer satisfaction • Lifetime value of a customer • Customer retention
Culture	New product culture: open to new ideas, experimentation	Relationship management culture: searching for more customer needs to satisfy
Most important customer	Most advanced customer	Most profitable, loyal customer
Priority-setting basis	Portfolio of products	Portfolio of customers—customer profitability
Main offering	Specific products	Personalized packages of service, support, education, consulting
Approach to personnel	Power to people who develop products • Highest reward is working on next most challenging product • Manage creative people through challenges with a deadline	Power to people with in-depth knowledge of customer's business • Highest rewards to relationship managers who save the customer's business
Sales bias	On the side of the seller in a transaction	On the side of the buyer in a transaction

fee or give Amazon some of its equity (or both) before it can access Amazon's 20 million proven Internet shoppers.

The argument thus far has painted the extremes of product and customer centricity. Not every company will need to go all the way with full customer centricity. The main point is that in most businesses today, the forces of the business are requiring a more customer-centric orientation. This orientation is achieved by creating organizational units for specific customers or customer segments and the leadership mind-sets to support them.

Lateral Networking Capability

To create multiproduct solutions for global customers, a company must work through lateral networks. A simple company with a few local customers selling a single product can work through a functional hierarchy. But a company with multiple product lines in multiple countries using multiple functions must work less through hierarchy and manage more through networks. Indeed a company needs a network for each strategically important dimension. Some companies like ABB have organized around global product lines. They have created country and functional networks to coordinate across product lines. Other companies like Nestlé have organized around country and regional profit centers. They have created product and functional networks to coordinate across the geographical structure. With the rise in importance of the customer dimension, there is now a need for a customer network across the product lines, countries, and functions.

The organization design decision, as described in Chapter Four, is to match the right kind of network with the strategic importance of the customer dimension. The types of lateral focus shown in Figure 4.3 will be applied in this section and the next chapter.

Informal or Voluntary

Nestlé is an example of informal networks formed around global customers. Unlike P&G, Nestlé has not strategically focused on

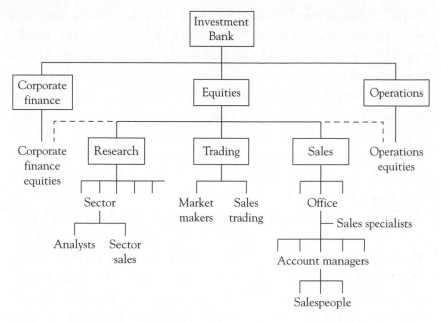

FIGURE 7.1. Equities Division Structure.

cross-border customers such as Carrefour or Wal-Mart. However, Nestlé country managers and country account managers for Wal-Mart routinely exchange information and ideas about Wal-Mart on an informal basis. This informal exchange is judged to be quite sufficient for Nestlé to deal with the global customer. Nestlé is a product-centric company and chooses to remain so.

E-Coordination

The equities division of a large investment bank (shown in Figure 7.1) provides an example e-coordination used to serve the customer. Equities has two shared units, one shared with corporate finance and the other with operations. The unit shared with corporate finance deals with the corporate customer and underwrites and originates equity offerings when the customer wants to tap the capital markets for funds. Of the three units that are wholly within equities, research assesses value of stocks and works with the corporate finance unit to evaluate and price new issues, and also provides recommendations to the sales unit, which sells stocks to institutional investors like mutual funds. The sales group calls on institutional investors to buy the equity issues originated by corporate finance and equities available on stock exchanges. When an institutional investor decides to buy or sell a stock, the trading unit executes the trade. The other shared unit, operations, completes the trade and settles with the parties to transactions. The relationship with the institutional investing customer involves effective e-coordination.

The equities division earns its revenue by executing trades for the institutional investor and receiving a commission on these trades. But almost every investment bank can execute trades. The challenge for the equities division is to earn the trades of the Fidelitys and Putnams of the world. It can do this in three ways. First, if the corporate finance unit can win the issuance of good stocks from good companies, the mutual funds will give the equities unit trades so as to get their fair share of these new stocks. Second, if the research unit provides the fund managers with good investing recommendations, the mutual fund will reward them with trades. Third, if the whole organization can provide superior, customized service, the customer will conduct more trades through the investment bank that has this capability.

The investment bank has chosen to pursue the superior service route in addition to attractive offerings and valuable research. The definition of superior service has changed in recent years. Originally, good service involved the transfer of privileged information. Today however, all market participants have access to the same information via Reuters or Bloomberg's on-line services. Superior service has become delivering interactive, customized service. Superior service has also required a new interactive approach to organizing around the customer.

Figure 7.2 illustrates the original organization and relationship management approach. The account manager owned the relationship. All communication with the customer went through the

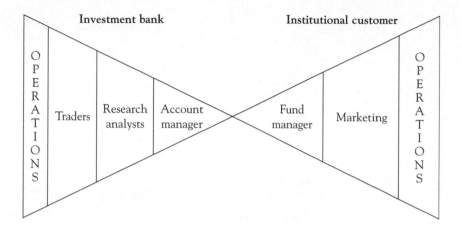

FIGURE 7.2. The Traditional Bow Tie.

account manager to the fund manager across the knot of the bow tie. Today changes at the customer have changed the bow tie to the pyramid shown in Figure 7.3. The mutual fund customer has grown and consolidated. Today the funds have their own small research group and traders. The equities division itself has many more specialists. As a result, the communication is now directly between the account manager and the fund manager and also between the other units and their counterparts. The challenge is to present an integrated offering to the mutual fund on terms that are desired by the fund. The equities division has chosen to serve its best customers via a Customer Relationship Management (CRM) system on the Web.

The leadership has selected forty key customers to receive the service. These are the largest customers and those who are most likely to value the service. The account manager for these customers prepares a quarterly plan with goals and objectives and places it on the CRM system. The plan is prepared based on input from key participants from the other functions who serve the customer. These are the analysts and sector sales people from research, the sales traders, and the liaison from operations. These people all

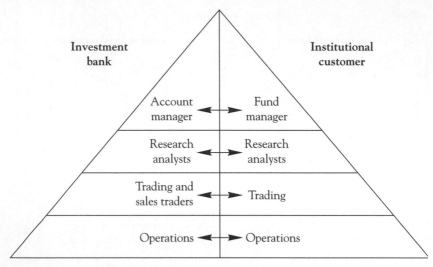

FIGURE 7.3. The Interactive Pyramid.

have access to the plan as well as to in-depth customer information. The customer's strategy, organization, and key contacts are all available on the system. The system records all transactions and transactions in progress with the customer. Everyone can get a good picture of the bank's business with these high-priority customers.

One of the purposes of the CRM system is to help the account manager manage the daily interactions between people at the customer and at the equities division. The daily interaction with the customer begins with the morning meeting. The group gathers on the sales floor and trading floor for the half-hour meeting. The meeting is conducted by the research unit, which presents the day's stock recommendations and the logic behind them. These recommendations will be those going to clients today. Then when trading begins, the people from sales and sector sales begin calling the fund managers and analysts at the funds. The notes from the morning meeting are on their screens along with talking points to be made with clients. An electronic ticker runs along the bottom of the screen showing prices and activity for the stocks mentioned in the meeting. There are links to research reports for these same stocks.

The salespeople record their calls to the customers. There is a chat window designed to record customer reactions to the recommendations and to serve as a running commentary throughout the day. The intent is to record people's observations and results of conversations with customers. The account manager gets a complete view of the evolving situation with the customer and can take whatever actions may be necessary.

The account managers learn from the CRM system and from their personal interactions with the customer. They customize the service on this basis. They learn that one client values direct conversations between the fund's analysts and the bank's analysts. The account manager then goes to the analysts to encourage them to spend time with the analysts at this top priority customer. Through the CRM systems, the manager can see if these conversations are happening. Another customer relies on its own analysts. Its managers believe that their fund has developed its own proprietary tools and analytical techniques. But the fund values the database used by the equities division's analysts. So the account manager and the research unit make this data available to the customer on the division's Web site. The customer's analysts can then access this data through their dedicated home page on the bank's Web site. The data is in a form that can be directly downloaded into the spreadsheets of the fund's analysts. Still another customer prefers direct interaction with the management of the company whose stock it is buying. The account manager makes sure this customer is invited to the division's conferences, provides copies of management speeches in written, voice, or video form, arranges visits through the corporate finance unit, and so on. Other customers value the interactions with the traders. The account manager influences the traders to deliver the services that the customer desires. Still other customers value rapid, flawless settlement of orders by the operations unit. Again the account manager arranges the necessary service and interactions.

The account manager today is less of a salesperson and more of a manager of the total relationship between the equities division and the top-priority customer. But most of the people serving the customers do not work for the account managers. How do they influence these other people in other departments? First, the customers help. The large funds usually rank the services received from the equities divisions of the investment banks they deal with, including the banks' research, trading, and operations execution. The funds will weight the rankings according to what is important to them. These rankings are used for bonus determination at the equities division. The account managers use these rankings to set goals for serving the customer and for influencing the other departments to meet the goals.

The equities division also has its own internal ranking system. The account managers provide ratings to all people in all departments with whom they work. These ratings are gathered quarterly and go into the rankings of the departments for their annual bonus determination. Actually, the analysts, traders, and operations staff also rate each other and the salespeople with whom they interact. These ratings are automated and come with thought-starters for the rating categories. The ratings are seen as the key incentive to encourage the cross-departmental cooperation needed to serve the customer.

The CRM system is a key tool in managing the interaction with the customer. The challenge is to get people to use it. The equities division's experience is like that of most companies in this regard. Everyone has gone through a training session explaining the system. The session also explains the practice of key account management, the customers' ranking system, and the division's rating system. The division then uses a mixture of carrots and sticks to encourage people to use the system. Its leaders are continually trying to improve the system itself. They try to make it easy to use and to deliver value to the user. The leaders and the account managers monitor who uses the system. They encourage people to use it and demonstrate how to get value from it. Clearly, the more people who use the system, the more valuable it is to everyone.

In summary, the equities division is a good example of the use of e-coordination to manage the interactions between the division and its top-priority customers. In simpler days, the interaction took place through the account manager. But today there are too many specialists both in the division and at the customers. The account manager could become a bottleneck. More effective conversations and interactions can take place between the specialists on both sides. The account manager now manages those interactions so that they are part of an effective relationship. The CRM system, the personal relationships, the customers' rankings, the division's ratings, the training program, and leadership encouragement all reinforce the e-coordination practice.

Formal Customer Teams

Formal customer teams are the next stronger level of coordination to be applied to serving customers. Usually this level of strength is implemented when the customer wants more than informal coordination and when the supplier chooses a strategy to provide superior service. There are three levels of complexity that can be involved, depending on the type of partnership that the parties create.

Key Accounts Teams. A common practice is to create a team consisting of all the salespeople serving a major customer. These salespeople could come from all product lines and all geographies in which the customer is present. These teams usually have names such as major accounts, national accounts, global accounts, and so on. They present a single face to those customers who want to partner in this way. Usually this team prepares an account plan from which revenue targets for all the salespeople are derived. This team represents a more formal version of the practice used by the equities division in the preceding section.

Supply Chain Team. Another type of team occurs when customer and supplier partner along the supply chain. These teams include more functions along with sales, and they jointly manage more activities. Wal-Mart and P&G have such a relationship. P&G initially formed a team of its salespeople representing all products that P&G provided to Wal-Mart. The team was expanded to include manufacturing, distribution, marketing, information technology, and finance. This team of about eighty people from various functions from all product lines worked to synchronize the product and order flow from P&G factories to Wal-Mart warehouses, to minimize inventories and cut cycle times. Today, as Wal-Mart expands globally, this team consists of 250 people from different functions, product lines, and countries.

Product Development Team. Companies supplying the automotive OEMs such as Ford take another step and include the R&D function on the customer teams. These teams not only partner along the supply chain like P&G and Wal-Mart but also partner in the product development process as well. The purpose of these teams is to customize the supplier's products for the automotive customer. For example, one Tier One supplier to the automotive industry has integrated the star model for a customer-centric approach by establishing an organization and customer team management process that supports products from development onward.

The leaders of the Tier One supplier believe that their organization is one of their sources of competitive advantage. They have a formal structure like many companies and an extensive lateral organization. One of the lateral structures is built around customer teams.

Up until recently, the division was a functional structure, appropriate for a single business. Then the sales and marketing function was divided into three geographic business units for the Americas, Europe and South Africa, and Japan and Asia. The change represents their increasing global presence and priority given to emerging markets. The functions of manufacturing and R&D remain the same but are matrixed across the new business units. The structure is shown in Figure 7.4.

A key lateral organization is the customer team. There is one

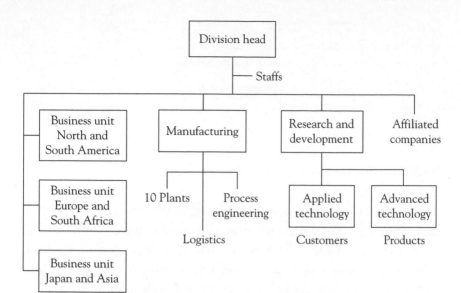

FIGURE 7.4. Organization of the Tier One Supplier.

team for each major OEM with whom the division works. The customer teams fit into the structure as shown in Figure 7.5.

They put the customer at the top of the structure. Then they have one layer between the customer and the executive committee (EC), which is made up of the division manager, the three business unit managers, and the manufacturing and R&D functional managers. Each customer team has a coach who is a member of the EC. The purpose is to allow rapid escalation of issues to the EC. The EC is the center for conflict resolution over priorities and disputes across teams.

Another EC issue is pricing. The teams coordinate prices for each automaker worldwide. That is, the price for Volkswagen in Germany must be coordinated with prices for Volkswagen in Brazil, China, and Mexico. Prices are adjusted for shipping, imports, duties, and taxes. Thus the price is not identical but must be coordinated for all customer locations.

The main purpose of the customer team is to coordinate the design of the new products for new customer platforms. The Tier One wants to get close to its customers so as to get ahead of its

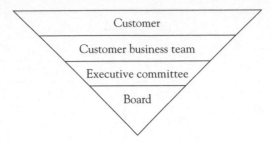

FIGURE 7.5. Customer at the Top of the Structure.

competitors. Its leaders want to be able to anticipate customer requirements. They need to know customer requirements three to five years in advance. They have a resident engineer or engineers at the customer site to learn what is going on. These resident engineers relay information to R&D. When a lead is discovered, R&D personnel start searching for solutions. They explore environmental impacts, resource availability, costs, and so on. They try to be better organized than their competitors on these issues. The goal is to be ahead of the customer and competitors. By knowing first and knowing better, they can prepare and get ahead. Then when the customer's management comes to them, they already have a project team in place and a set of alternatives prepared. When successful, they can even influence the customer's preferences.

A customer team is a combination of countries and functions, as illustrated in Figure 7.6. It consists of core team members and extended team members. The core team consists of the sales and marketing representatives from each country in which the customer is present and makes buying decisions. They are in contact with the customer every day. Other core team members are functional representatives from the country in which the customer is based. The decision center for the customer is in the home country. The team leader usually comes from the applied technology function, which is itself organized by customer. The sales and marketing representative could also be the team leader. In the customer's home country, the applied technology engineer and the sales and marketing rep-

	Brazil	Germany	North America	China
Sales and marketing	X	X	X	X
Applied technology		LEADER		
R&D		X		
Manufacturing	V	X	V	V
Logistics		X		
Quality		X		

X = member of core team
V = member of extended team

FIGURE 7.6. Customer Team at Volkswagen.

resentative are 100 percent dedicated to the customer. The extended team members are functional representatives from other countries in which the customer is present. They become active when building or adding to a plant, introducing a new product, or creating the business plan.

Business planning is done by customer and by the business team. The teams prepare a plan for each customer engine by engine, process by process, country by country, and function by function. They make a list of all future opportunities and a list of problem areas. The Tier One stresses the norms of not hiding problems. Problems are to be solved—not to generate punishment. Priorities are set and programs are initiated or continued. These plans are reviewed and updated quarterly versus goals, milestones, and strategies. The teams are measured by customer share.

The customer teams were started five years ago. The company began with one team for Daimler Benz. The people, particularly those from sales, were initially fearful. But as problems were solved, people began to see the benefits and to enjoy the teamwork. The cost was time taken from functional jobs. Other teams were added. The company has always experimented with the teams. It has tried electing team leaders, rotating the leader role, and finally settled on selecting them. The leader role is now evaluated higher and people want the opportunity.

Currently there is concern about competition between the customer teams. The Tier One has always allowed some competition between its customer teams. Sometimes the request comes from the customers. Currently there are two dedicated teams working on similar projects for different customers. The two teams are developing different solutions for the same application. Both teams have signed nondisclosure agreements. The leaders of the teams stay informed. They will prevent failures but will allow different solutions. When not restricted these leaders are the links between teams and the means of spreading best practices. The EC recently had a meeting and a discussion with the team leaders about the current competitive situation. The EC is discussing what steps to take to maintain a balance. So the leadership is constantly monitoring and improving the performance of the team process.

Some formal processes are used to develop the appropriate goals and performance measures. The key is the planning process, which takes place around customers and is created by the customer teams. These plans result in programs for the teams and in goals and milestones for the team members. The teams are measured on the share of the customer's business they win.

The plans and the actual performance of the customer teams are added up for the regional business units (RBUs). The RBUs are then evaluated on the basis of a measure similar to earnings before interest and taxes (EBIT) for each OEM headquartered in the region. The diagram shown in Figure 7.7 illustrates the situation. The RBU manager for the Americas is measured on the global profitability of General Motors and Ford. So revenues and costs, no matter where they accrue, are assigned to customers' accounts. The RBU manager for Europe is responsible for the global profitability of Volkswagen, DaimlerChrysler, Renault, and other companies based in that region. The RBUs are not just regional entities but are globally responsible for their locally headquartered customers. The

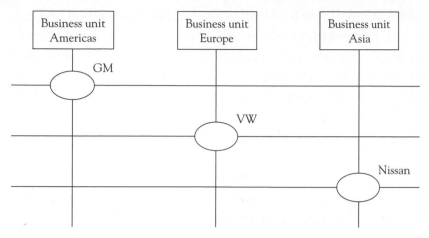

FIGURE 7.7. Customer Profitability Responsibility.

customer team leaders also have an allegiance to the RBU manager as well as to their function. The country managers of the sub-sidiaries are still measured on a country P&L. They serve all cus-tomers in their countries. These measures add a constant tension to the country-region relation.

The HR processes reinforce the customer teams. They are geared toward selecting, developing, and rewarding people who like the customer team value system. The leaders search for people who can overcome the hierarchy. They give a realistic job preview and use peer interviewing. The current leader took over fifteen years ago when there were 120 people. Today there are 712. So the company has largely selected and developed its own talent.

The Tier One believes the opportunity for travel and interna-tional experience attracts people to it. To attain a position in top management, a manager must work a minimum of four years abroad. This view is discussed up front with potential candidates and is enforced.

The EC members go over the list of top people and assess them, engaging in an open discussion about all the managers. They rank people within functions and across functions. They are believers in the ranking process and the discussion that it produces. All EC members are deeply involved in the business; they travel and collect data constantly and know the management population. People are assessed on their total contribution. They do not want just a superior engineer. (Nonetheless, they have places for superior engineers.) They want a good total contributor. They are particularly interested in *social competence*—defined as being able to go out for a beer with someone after having had a good fight in the business meeting. The ranking discussion flushes out these people as well as establishes the criteria for judging. These rankings are the basis for assessments, bonuses, and promotions. The leaders also spend time seeing that the organization and interdepartmental relationships are healthy. Traditionally in their business the interface between R&D and manufacturing has been the tension point. As a result the members of the EC have worked to make sure that both units are aware of each other's problems and appreciate the issues. They hold regular workshops where both groups are in attendance. These workshops focus on product teams, new product programs, and especially improvements in the product development process. Out of these workshops have come ideas for rotational assignments for those who are interested and for co-locating groups in each other's departments. The workshops are attended by members of the EC. They are held over two days so that the groups can spend social time together and get to know one another.

The role of the leadership is central to the success of the customer teams. The division leader and the EC members are very active and visible within the division. Their purpose is to demonstrate the customer team values. In addition to the EC meetings already described, they hold "Information Days" once or twice a year. They visit each plant and R&D site and meet with all employees. The purpose is to spend equal time explaining what's happening in the business and listening to the views and questions of the people. Every quarter they present all the financial figures to everyone at the sites. They want to create an open system where all information is visible.

The EC and its members try to live the company values. Issues involving customers, regions, and functions are discussed in the EC, which meets once a month for about twelve hours. These meetings are described as being "heated." Conflicts are surfaced and debated. The goal is to quickly recognize issues that cannot be resolved in customer teams, product teams, and project teams—and to resolve them.

In summary, the leadership of the Tier One has developed the three capabilities to deliver itself to its customers wherever they happen to be. The company has a customer-centric capability, a capability to use lateral relationships, and a mind-set that organization is an advantage that competitors cannot easily duplicate.

The Tier One takes the team one step further and includes R&D participation. The company's salespeople coordinate across borders to serve DaimlerChrysler and other automakers the way ABB serves its customers. It also partners along the supply chain to synchronize production with the DaimlerChrysler assembly lines the way P&G coordinates with Wal-Mart. But its engineers also determine DaimlerChrysler's new product needs and coordinate with DaimlerChrysler personnel on creating new catalysts for new automotive platforms. The Tier One creates customer-specific, platform-specific catalysts for exhaust emissions.

So these formal customer networks can vary from a few key account teams for salespeople to supply chain partnership teams of sales, logistics, and other functional people to new product development teams that include all functions including the various types of engineering. For some companies like the Tier One, this customer team organization is sufficient to meet the needs of its most important customer. Other companies choose to take a further step of creating a full-time coordinator to manage all customer team activities.

Customer Accounts Coordinator

The next step in conferring more power to the customer dimension is the creation of an integrating role for the customer accounts and teams. When a company grows fifty or more teams and customers want still more coordination from a supplier, the key account or global account coordinator role is a useful addition to the informal networks and formal customer teams. The coordinator provides three new factors.

First the coordinator becomes a voice for the customer on the management team. These teams usually consist of managers of product lines, geographies, and functions. The coordinator gets the leadership thinking in terms of a portfolio of customers, customer priorities, and customer centricity. Customer teams can also appeal to the coordinator in resolving conflicts.

The second task of the coordinator is to build and manage the infrastructure to support customer teams. The formal communications were mentioned earlier. The coordinators would assume the role of managing customer information systems and communications across customer teams. They usually create training programs for management and team members on the role and operation of key accounts. Many coordinators create a common planning system for customer plans. If fifty customer teams are creating plans, they are likely to create fifty planning formats. The coordinators simplify and speed up the process by agreeing on a single common format.

Another key addition to the infrastructure is a customer accounting system leading to customer P&Ls. Customer profitability is a key measure in setting customer priorities. In addition, asymmetries in costs and revenues always occur across geographies. That is, the customer account manager and team in the customer's home country put in extra efforts to make a sale to their customer. Often the initiative is successful but the customer's first purchases are for its subsidiaries in other countries. Thus the costs are incurred in the home country and the revenues are booked in other countries. A global accounting system for customers can identify these asymmetries and management can correct for them.

The third addition is to provide industry expertise. When the number of major accounts grows, companies usually group them by industry. For example, Citibank grew its global accounts to around 250 and then grouped them into about ten industry groups. This specialization allows for the accumulation of more in-depth knowledge of the customers. All these infrastructure additions can be combined in the planning process. The countries and product lines can then set customer-specific goals for key accounts, allowing customer teams, countries, and product lines to pursue an aligned set of goals.

Matrix Organization

The next step in enhancing the power base of the customer dimension is to form customer- or customer segment–dedicated units within countries and product lines and have them report to the customer coordinator. The assumption is that the customer dimension has attained a strategic importance equal to the countries or business units. This importance is expressed by making the customer organization an equal partner in the decision-making process. In countries where the company may not control 100 percent of the equity, joint ventures to serve multinational clients are often created between the parent company and local subsidiary.

This chapter has described the forces that are driving companies to organize around the customer. This customer dimension is added to the existing product, geography, and function structures. The next chapter shows how some companies are actually creating profit centers around customers or customer segments.

8

Customer-Focused Structures

Many of the companies mentioned in the preceding chapter, like Citibank and Procter & Gamble, started with customer teams and then evolved into structural units dedicated to customers and customer segments. These customer segments then evolved into profit centers. The result is a hybrid structure referred to as the *front/back model*. Both P&G and Citibank grew a customer-centric unit and added it to the product profit centers. These customer-facing units are the front end of the business. The original product lines are the back end. The leadership challenge is to link the new front end with the old back end.

The Front/Back Hybrid Structure

The front/back hybrid is a combination of product and market structures. It consists of a front-end structure that is focused on market segments or geography (or both) and a back-end structure that is focused on products and technologies. Both the front and back ends are multifunctional structures in themselves.

The front/back structure is shown in Figure 8.1, which illustrates a financial services firm that offers insurance, mutual fund, and savings certificate products. The products are organized as multifunctional businesses including every function except for sales. They form the product-focused back-end structure. The front-end

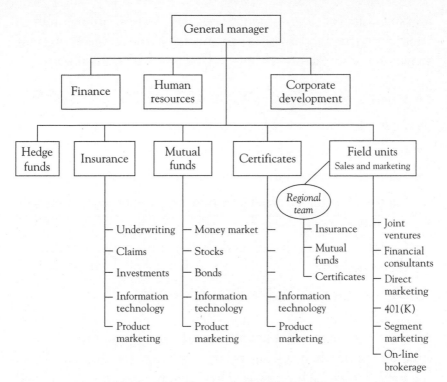

FIGURE 8.1. Front/Back Structure for Financial Services.

structure consists of multiple sales channels, segment marketing, and regional coordination units that link the products and channels. Five thousand financial consultants are geographically dispersed. They provide financial advice and sell investment products. Direct mail and 800 numbers represent other distribution channels. The company recently trained financial consultants for companies offering 401(K) plans to their employees. All products are sold through all channels.

Successful execution of the front/back structure gives a company great flexibility. The aim is to focus the business both on markets and products so as to achieve the benefits of both product and market structures. A number of forces at play in the market today have combined to cause companies to choose this organization type. Variety, change, and speed encourage companies to adopt fast-moving units based on product lines. But several other forces in addition to the standard ones can encourage the addition of a customer or market focus—a front-end focus—to a product focus:

- Customers buy all products.
- Customers want a single contact point.
- Customers want a sourcing relationship.
- Customers want solutions, not components.
- Customer demands provide opportunities for cross-selling and bundling.
- Customers want products and services customized to meet their needs.
- Customer knowledge is a distinct advantage.

The pressure for a market focus, and a corresponding front-end structure, starts when customers buy—or can buy—all products. (If the products are each purchased by different customers, there will be no pressure for a front-end structure.) When customers are buying all products, it becomes awkward for each product group to have its own sales force, all of which call on the same customer. Would it not be more economical to have one sales force sell all products to the customer? In part, the answer depends on how the customer wants to do business. Some customers have different buyers purchasing different products from the same vendor. These companies may prefer to have separate product-knowledgeable salespeople calling on separate product-knowledgeable buyers. But more customers today prefer to pool their purchases and negotiate total single contracts with multiproduct vendors. These customers want a single contact in each vendor organization with whom they can communicate and negotiate. The need for these single interfaces for customers is a force in the creation of the front-end structure.

Many customers today are adopting sourcing policies. That is, they prefer to have fewer, closer, and longer-term vendor relationships. They choose one or two vendors for a product and dedicate their entire volume to those vendors. In return, the customer may prefer—or insist—that the vendor create an organizational unit with which it can conduct its business. This unit becomes a front-end unit.

Some customers want to buy solutions rather than stand-alone products. This shaping force was described in Chapter Seven.

On some occasions, there may be cross-selling opportunities for the vendor with customers who do not buy all the vendor's products. By packaging (or *bundling*) products together for a single package price, the vendor may win a larger share of the customer's business. Cross-selling and bundling usually require a single unit in the front end to create the package for the customer.

These examples show that more value-adding activities are being done and are best located in the front-end structure. In the past, sales was the only activity organized around the customer. Today, more customer-specific software and services are being added. PPG used to sell paint to automobile manufacturers, for example. Today, it sells paint, provides application software for choosing paints, and runs the entire painting operation for General Motors.

As the economies of developed countries become service and information oriented, companies will continue to add software and services as a source of growth. These services usually require customization for market segments and customers. As a result, they should be located in the front-end structure.

Finally, many companies are recognizing that a market segment structure allows them to gain superior knowledge about customers and to form close relationships with them. If the knowledge and relationships can be converted into superior products and services, the segment focus will become a competitive advantage. The total benefits to the successfully executed front/back organization are those achieved by both market and product structures.

Four important design issues must be resolved in creating a front/back organization:

- Placement of marketing
- Roles and responsibilities
- Problems of contention
- Front/back linkage

The question of whether to put marketing in the front or the back end always comes up. As it turns out, marketing goes in both places. Segment or customer marketing goes in the front, focusing on segmenting the customer population. It concentrates on creating packages of products and services for segments, package pricing, channel selection, and supporting the sales force. Product marketing goes in the back, focusing on product positioning, product pricing, new product development, and product features. The two marketing activities will play key roles in linking the front and back, as later examples illustrate.

The second design issue involves the respective roles and responsibilities of the front and the back. If these roles are not clarified, there is great potential for conflict. Just about every management decision can create contention. Who sets price? Who forecasts? Who is responsible for the inventory? The most contentious question is, Which end is the profit center? Some managements wish to emphasize one or the other. However, it is possible to design both to be profit centers, and manage them with a spreadsheet planning process like the one shown in Exhibit 5.1.

The third issue is managing contention. Even if the roles and responsibilities are acceptable, there is bound to be some contention. The front end sees the world through market eyes and wants unique things for its customers. The back end sees the world through product eyes and wants scale and equal customer treatment. The discussion of the customer-centric and product-centric thinking in Chapter Seven is typical of these inevitable conflicts. Management needs to create processes for using conflict to learn about customers and products, and for resolving issues in a timely fashion.

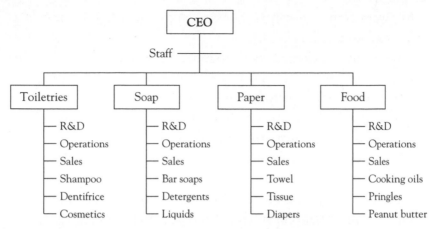

FIGURE 8.2. Group Structure of Procter & Gamble.

Finally, management needs to link the front with the back for key work flow processes. Orders need to enter the front and be filled at the back. Products need to be developed by the back and sold by the front. The two types of structures should not lead to two companies. Tight linkage is necessary despite the inherent conflicts. Management's time and effort in resolving conflicts and linking the front and the back are the major costs of implementing this model.

Procter & Gamble's Front/Back Model

P&G provides an excellent example of the structures and lateral processes needed for successful execution of the front/back model. Consumer goods manufacturing companies were originally structured around categories, as shown in Figure 8.2. In the late 1980s, P&G's retail customers began to change. The volume buying and intelligence acquired through check-out counter bar code scanners at such mass merchandisers as Wal-Mart and Kmart substantially increased their power. Some of them demanded a single interface, along with just-in-time supply relationships. In contrast, other retailers began to experience considerable variety in the buying habits of ethnic groups within the regions they served. These retailers were moving in the opposite direction from the mass merchants.

They were doing less central buying, even moving the buying decisions to the store level.

Consumer packaged goods manufacturers have responded differently to these forces. P&G tried to acquire an advantage by adding a front-end structure that enables responsiveness to all types of customers. This structure is shown in Figure 8.3, which illustrates that both a regional structure and a customer structure have been created as the front end of the business. The regional and customer teams are all multifunctional and staffed by people who come from the product groups. Customer teams are created for customers large enough to justify the effort who want to coordinate operations very closely. Some customer teams are located at the customer headquarters. The teams consist of several functions. First there are the marketing people, who work with customer marketing on analyzing bar code data and using promotions to move product. Then there are the salespeople, who talk directly to the buyers at the customer's merchandising functions. Next there are distribution and information technology people, who link the logistics functions of the producer and the retailer. Sometimes factory people join the teams to discuss putting on bar codes and prices in the factory rather than in the stores. Financial people on both sides discuss ways to speed the turnover of inventory and accounts receivable and minimize cash.

The whole cross-functional team works for a customer team leader, who is a senior manager from either sales or marketing. The leader of the entire front end is a senior manager with sales and marketing experience.

Product coordination within a customer team is accomplished by the team leader and the top functional managers, and by cross-functional teams for each product group. The product team is chaired by the marketing representative. All the product group functional representatives in the front end also communicate with their counterparts in the product groups. These representatives are on two- to three-year rotational assignment from the product groups. Their contacts within the group are kept current throughout the rotations. But in each case, there is a clearly defined

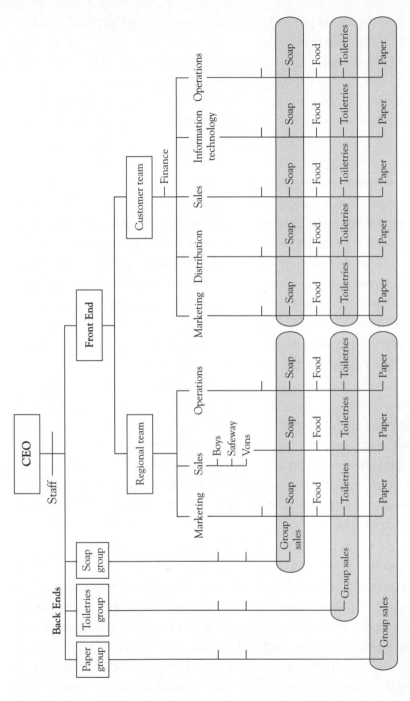

FIGURE 8.3. Front-End Structure of Procter & Gamble.

interface between products and customers, using the product representatives in the front end.

The regional teams consist of three functions. The marketing function translates the product marketing message into regional versions. The sales function consists of teams that call on stores where the buying decisions are located. In Southern California, for example, customers large enough to justify a team are such retailers as Boys Market and Vons. One store in Monterey Park serves a largely Taiwanese population. Products must appeal to ethnic Chinese and be in Chinese packaging. The same retailer in Malibu serves the specialized beach community with health foods. The local variety of customers requires responsiveness on a local level. The operations function works with the stores' operations people to set up displays and stock shelves. The functional people on regional teams also can form product teams and communicate with their counterparts in the product groups.

Some customers prefer to do business as they have in the past. For these customers, the company sends salespeople from the group sales forces. The soap salespeople talk to the soap buyers; the paper salespeople talk to the paper buyers. So sales staff can be organized by group (as they have been traditionally), by region, or by customer. The company has maintained product specialization at the salesperson level, but it has organized them simultaneously by product group, region, and customer. A rotational assignment process develops them to see all three sides of the issue and maintain personal networks.

One strength of this front/back design is that it allows the company to do business *the way the customer wants to do business*. Different customers prefer different relationships. Another strength of the design is the clear identification of product people and product teams in the front end. These groups can communicate and coordinate within the front end and between the front end and the back end. The structure makes it easy for the customer, but it can be complex for the producer. The same conflicts described earlier exist between customer teams and product lines. In addition, the different interfaces with different customers make things difficult to coordinate. But if the company can manage the conflict and the complexity, it will have achieved a competitive advantage. Competitors cannot easily copy and execute the entire front/back organization.

Building a Customer-Centric Capability

Most companies grow a customer-centric capability and add it to their product and geographic structures. This section describes how professional service (PS) firms have grown their customer-centric units. Good examples are the investment banks like Citigroup and UBS Warburg and the systems integrators like Accenture and EDS. Most of the large multinational PS firms saw that they were in a position to serve global customers. But they needed to change their country-based organizations and skeptical country managers and to build a capability to coordinate across countries. Their change process was a systematic progression through the lateral forms, starting simple and getting increasingly complex.

Step 1: A Few Customer Teams

An initial step to drive the change was to create approximately five customer teams to serve the customer around the world. Care was taken to choose the five customers that were most desirous of this global service. The account manager serving the customer's headquarters was the team leader. In each country where the customer wanted service, one team member was selected. This team then put together an integrated customer strategy and plan to serve the customer—and executed it. Two things usually resulted from this effort. One was the intended purpose of better coordination across countries to deliver integrated service to the global customer. The second was the opportunity to drive organizational change and build organizational capability.

The first opportunity is provided by satisfied customers. They can become a genuine force for change. If they were carefully selected, these customers should respond positively to any efforts to better serve them across countries. They will probably respond positively but they will also indicate that more effort is needed to meet their needs. This outside force—a satisfied customer wanting more—can be used to change country-focused mind-sets. The request for more effort makes the customer part of the change process.

Then there is the opportunity to expand and build upon the capability already created. With each customer team consisting of 50 to 60 people, between 250 and 300 people have now become aware of and part of the change effort. There are now 300 people trained in cross-border customer strategies. There are 300 people who now understand the needs of the global customer. There are 300 people who now have cross-border networks and personal contacts. The 300 people themselves will have had different experiences. Most of them should be positive if people were chosen and recruited on the basis of skills and interests. They too can become a positive force for change. Some of these people will enjoy the experience and want more. Some will find that serving local clients is more to their liking and can opt out. For the observant management, the effort is an audition to find cross-border talent. Some people will be good at this new effort and others not. Those managements that see their task as identifying new leadership will use the teams as an opportunity to do so. And finally, the effort provides an experience from which to learn and improve. By collecting team members' and customers' experiences and ideas, the customer team effort can be improved next time.

In this manner every change to the formal structure and systems creates two outcomes. The first is to improve the execution of some task. This outcome remains the intended purpose of the change. But a second outcome is the opportunity for management to engage customers in a closer relationship with the company, change mindsets of the doubters, train agents of change, build personal networks, select and develop new leaders, and improve the process. For those managements that capture the opportunity, they can use changes to the formal structure and lateral forms to drive and shape organizational change. These two outcomes are produced at each step in the sequence.

Step 2: More Customer Teams

A next step would be to expand from a handful of teams to a dozen or so teams. Again the firm selects those customers who want the integrated service. The firm can also solicit volunteers or carefully select team members who are interested in cross-border work. The initial team members can solicit their colleagues to join. Usually the firm can make these team assignments attractive. In professional service firms, people are interested in personal growth and opportunity. Working on a team serving a global customer can be a source of learning and development not available with local clients. The multinational customer is usually the most advanced customer. Management can also follow up to see that working on global customer teams is recognized and rewarded in the countries.

Similar outcomes should result from this expanded effort. The difference from the first phase is the larger number of people involved. Instead of a few hundred, this time a thousand or more people are trained in serving global customers and building their networks. A couple of dozen customers are satisfied and asking for more. A critical mass of change agents is being built.

Step 3: Global Accounts Coordinator

The next step is to create a position on the management team to coordinate the efforts to serve the global customer. At a minimum this change creates a voice or a champion on the management team for the global customer. Someone of higher status can now appeal to recalcitrant country managers. The coordinator will expand the number of teams again. But perhaps most important, this role can fund and build a customer-focused infrastructure.

One task is to create a common process for building global customer plans and strategies. Initially some experimenting by customer teams is useful. But soon the countries get overwhelmed with fifteen different planning formats. The coordinator can collect best practices from the various teams, initiate a task force staffed with veterans of global teams, and create common guidelines, forms, and processes. The common process makes it easier for customer teams and country management to work together.

The next step is the design and building of customer-based information and accounting systems. The question always arises, "Are we making any money serving these global customers?" With country-based accounting systems and profit centers, it is usually impossible to tell. Depending on whether the countries have compatible systems or not, this change can be a major effort requiring central funding and leadership from the global account coordinator. But in the end, the customer teams have information with which to measure their progress, compare their performance with other teams, and demonstrate global profitability.

The two steps can be combined by generating revenue and profit targets for customers in the planning process. The teams can have revenue and profit goals for their global customers. The teams can have goals for revenue and profit in each country. Perhaps more important, the goals can be added up in each country. Then each country manager can have revenue and profit goals for local clients and global accounts. The country managers can get credit for—and be held accountable for—targets for global customers in their countries. The accounting system is important because the costs and revenues from the global customer are rarely connected. For example, an account team in the London office of one of the Big Five worked for a year to win the global audit of a big U.K. firm. They were successful—but most of the work for the next few years would be in the North American subsidiary and in a recent acquisition in Australia. That means that the work plus the costs to win the business were incurred in the U.K. and the revenues were booked in North America and Australia. With customer profit accounting, the U.K.

can identify the revenues and costs and receive credit. The targets can be adjusted for these disconnects. Thus in addition to being a champion for the customer, the global accounts coordinator can create the processes and information systems to manage the global customer as well as continue to develop and identify talent and leadership on the teams.

Step 4: A Global Accounts Group

As the number of global accounts and teams exceeds several hundred the global accounts coordinator role can be expanded into a department or a group. In part for ease of supervision, the customers and teams are grouped into broadly defined industry categories like consumer products, financial services, oil and gas, pharmaceuticals and life sciences, multimedia, and so on. But the main reason is customer satisfaction. Customers want auditors and consultants who understand their business. Bankers do not want to teach their auditors about derivatives. Pharmaceutical companies assume their consultants know what the Human Genome Project is all about. So the global accounts activity can be expanded and specialized by customer segment.

The global accounts leadership usually leads an effort to establish a common segmentation scheme across the company. In large countries like Germany, the United Kingdom, and Japan, customer segments were probably already in use. What is important is to have compatible schemes across the countries. Then a one-to-one interface can be established to facilitate communication between countries and within an industry.

The global accounts group is usually expanded by adding global industry coordination. A global industry coordinator is selected for each industry that is common across the countries. Many companies realize the need for global coordinating roles but find few people qualified to fill the roles. But if a company has followed the advice presented in this chapter and used the opportunity created by the initial customer team implementations, it should have grown its own talent by this point.

An audit firm can serve as an example. A young Swiss auditor was identified as a talented performer on audits of banks in Zurich. When a global team was created for Citibank, the auditor, who had experience in audits of Citibank's subsidiary, became the Swiss representative on the Citibank team. Based on good performance, the auditor agreed to an assignment in the United Kingdom. The move gave the auditor the opportunity to work in the London financial center. While in London, the auditor served as the U.K. representative on the Credit Swiss global team. The next assignment was to lead an in-depth audit of the Credit Swiss–First Boston investment bank in the United States. The auditor was then made partner and returned to Zurich. From there he was selected to be the global account team leader for Credit Swiss. After several years in the team leader role, the auditor became the global coordinator for the financial services customer segment. The auditor was assessed in each assignment for audit performance and knowledge of the financial services industry as usual. But assessments were also made of teamwork, relationship with customers, ability to influence without authority, cross-cultural skills with customers, and cross-cultural skills and leadership of the cross-border team. Based on these experiences and training courses, the auditor was qualified to move into the global coordinator role.

Step 5: Global Accounts Units in Countries

A next step to shift more power to the teams serving global customers is to carve out units within countries and dedicate them to the global customers. The other country units will serve local customers. The global customer units report to the global accounts coordinator and to the local country manager. These country units place dedicated talent in the service of the global customer.

In some small countries, the country managers may be reluctant to create a dedicated unit and share in its direction. They may have a surplus of profitable local business and prefer to avoid the multinationals. In these cases several PS firms have created joint ventures between the headquarters and the local country management. Usually the dedicated unit is funded from headquarters and staffed initially with expatriates. Then after a couple of years, the local managers notice that the unit is quite profitable. In addition they notice that the unit is a positive factor in recruiting. Many new hires are attracted by the opportunity to work with global firms. In this way the creation of a global customer joint venture changes the mind-sets of local managers. They eventually take over the staffing and share in the administration of the unit.

Step 6: Customer Profit Centers

A final change is the creation of customers and customer segments as the line organization and profit centers. All the global units report to the global industry units. The countries manage the local business and serve as geographic coordinators.

A similar stepwise process was followed by Citibank's commercial banking business. Starting in 1985 Citibank reestablished its World Corporations Group, which managed global corporations across the country profit center structure. It created teams for each global account. The members were called subsidiary account managers and the leader was a principal account manager. The number of customers qualifying to become global accounts increased to around 450. Citibank created a customer-focused planning system and an accounting system to track customer revenue, cost, and profit across countries.

In 1995, Citibank conducted a strategy study and realized that it was in the business of taking deposits and making loans in over a hundred countries—more than double its nearest competitor (Hong Kong–Shanghai Bank, with around forty-three countries). This presence was a competitive advantage when serving the global customer and one that could not be matched by competitors. Citibank managers chose to emphasize the cross-border bank role. They would focus on global products, foreign exchange, and cash management for global customers. Each of thirteen hundred global

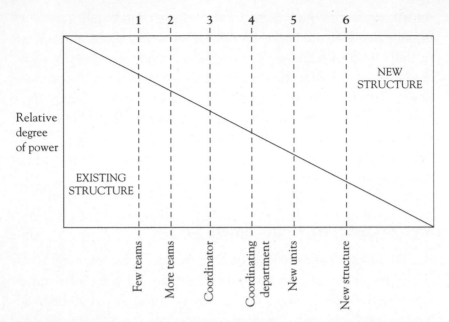

FIGURE 8.4. Shifting Power Incrementally to a New Structure.

customers became a profit center. These customers were collected into global industry groupings for administration. The customer-focused planning process is now called COMPASS and is placed on an intranet. Thus in about twelve years, Citibank evolved from country profit centers to customer profit centers. It evolved its strategy, structure, and systems. It drove the change with formal integrating mechanisms like customer teams and global account coordinators before completing it with the establishment of a new formal structure.

In general, management can drive a change process that transforms any existing organization into any new organization using the sequential approach. Each step in the sequence makes an incremental shift in the power structure. The incremental changes are shown in Figure 8.4.

Each increment corresponds to the change in the example. Starting with a few teams and moving to stronger coordinating units, the example described the transfer of power from countries (existing) to customers (new). At each step new work is accomplished. In the PS firms the new work was cross-country coordination to provide integrated service to the global customer. At each step there is also the opportunity to drive and shape the change process. With teams, Step 1 and Step 2, three hundred and then a thousand people learn about the global customer. They learn how to create strategies that competitors cannot match. A percentage of the participants will become convinced of the direction and lobby the nonbelievers. Through the teams, a thousand people are building networks of personal contacts.

Management's role is to seize the opportunity and drive the change. It may sponsor a formal development program. Everyone working on teams could spend several days in a session with their other team members. In addition to facilitating more learning and networking, managers and customer representatives could attend and get feedback from the participants. But most important is the opportunity for management to select and develop the talent and leadership for the new strategy and structure. By observing and reviewing the teams, management can identify those who have the skills and interest in cross-border work. Who are the best potential team members? Who can be a team leader? Who can develop into a global industry coordinator?

The coordinator roles, introduced and developed in Steps 3, 4, and 5, shift more power to the new structure and deliver more service to the customer. But the other opportunity is to develop processes and information systems to support the new organization. In addition, the coordinator teaches managers about the new strategy. They must shift from managing a portfolio of countries to managing a portfolio of customers. How will they make trade-offs and set priorities? Thus at each step management has the opportunity to change the soft factors to support the change. It can develop the talent, build the networks, change the mind-sets, and ultimately create a cross-border, customer-focused culture.

The ultimate step in organizing around the customer is to create a separate structural component for customers. Usually this capability in structural form is added to the company's existing structure creating a front/back hybrid. Managing this structural form creates its own challenge. Building this customer-centric capability is the other management challenge. The result is an ambidextrous organization generating both excellent products and customer focus.

9

Creating a Virtual Corporation

The virtual corporation, sometimes called the networked organization, is another form of organization that is becoming popular. It is created by extensive contracting out of activities once performed in-house. The new information technology facilitates the virtual corporation by allowing independent firms to join together in networks, which then act as if they are single corporations. There are some compelling reasons to choose the virtual corporation design, but there are also some negatives.

What Is a Virtual Corporation?

Virtual corporation is another fashionable term in the business press. The virtual corporation is sometimes defined by what it is not. It is the exact opposite of the vertically integrated corporation. Instead of covering all the activities a business comprises—from raw material to the ultimate consumer—the virtual corporation contracts out for all activities except those in which it is superior. As a result, a network of independent companies—each doing what it does best—acts together as if it were virtually a single corporation. Hence the name. But why is the virtual corporation popular?

When duly qualified, it is an option with considerable merit. The virtual corporation is a reflection of the trend to contracting out. The traditional corporate model was for a company to own and control all activities that created value for its customers. But today, companies recognize that they are not—and cannot be—best at everything. Yet in today's competitive market, it really is necessary to be best at everything. The virtual corporation can provide the answer, as companies perform what they do best and seek to acquire or become partners with other companies that do best at other parts of the job so as to get superior total offering for the customer.

Also favoring the virtual corporation is the issue of size. Some suggest that in today's economy—characterized by variety, change, and speed, as discussed in the other chapters of this book—size is no longer an advantage, and may even be a disadvantage. Some would say that the future belongs to the small, entrepreneurial niche firm. And, indeed, in an increasing number of situations small is beautiful. However, in some industries small niche firms are being taken over by larger firms with more scale and deeper pockets; in the automobile industry, Jaguar, Saab, and Mazda are examples. Peter Drucker has proposed a compromise by suggesting that medium is the best size. The medium-size firm is not too large to move quickly and not too small to get scale. He suggests that this medium-size firm is the real strength of German industry.

The virtual corporation provides the ultimate answer. It can be large when it is an advantage to be large and it can be small when it is an advantage to be small. For example, it is an advantage to be large when buying; volume discounts and better terms can be secured. Thus the independent companies within the virtual corporation can pool their purchases, and one company—usually the lead company—can buy for all companies. Benetton, the Italian fashion house, takes this approach. It contracts out most manufacturing to about 350 small firms and buys the materials for all of them. Benetton has become the world's largest purchaser of wool thread and exercises considerable leverage in that market. However, it is good to be small and independent when fast, flexible responses are called for. The labor-intensive fashion sewing and packing operations are performed for Benetton by twenty- to twenty-five–person firms. Collectively, these small companies can handle the variety and flexibility needed to supply rapidly changing fashion merchandise to a fickle market.

Thus the virtual corporation is able to gain scale without mass. Yet Benetton and other virtual corporations can be both large and small, depending on which is advantageous at the time.

Flexible sourcing is another advantage to using networks of independent firms. For example, in the past decade five different printing and four different storage technologies have been used for personal computers. By contracting out for components, Apple, Compaq, and Dell have avoided building a dot-matrix printer factory and a floppy disk drive factory. If flash memories replace hard disk drives, these manufacturers can quickly shift to the new storage devices by establishing a new source. The virtual corporation is thus an advantage in fast-moving, changing industries.

The virtual corporation is made possible largely by the new information technology. Benetton has designed an international telecom network that ties together all of its franchise stores and all of its subcontracted factories. Its 6,000 franchises and 350 factories interact via a worldwide telecommunications network that a Fortune 500 company would be proud to own. But instead of owning the franchises and factories, Benetton holds together the network through telecommunications and intelligence.

But the virtual corporation, like any organizational form, has its disadvantages. The greatest disadvantage is the possible loss of proprietary knowledge. To work with other companies, a company must exchange information. But when important information is given to others, potential competitors are created. For example, Apple taught independent software vendors about the Macintosh operating system so that they could write application programs that would run on the Mac. One of those vendors was Microsoft. Microsoft did, indeed, write programs for the Mac, but it also incorporated what it learned into its own operating system, Windows. Once Windows 3.0 appeared, Apple had lost its competitive advantage. Similarly, Schwinn contracted out its bicycle manufacturing to a Taiwanese firm. After learning the U.S. bicycle business, the

Taiwanese firm sidestepped Schwinn and went directly into distribution through mass merchandisers like Wal-Mart. Schwinn is just now emerging from Chapter 11.

Another disadvantage is that the more activities a firm contracts out, the more profit and value-added it gives to others. Conversely, the more things a firm is good at doing, the more value and profit it can keep to itself.

A third possible negative is loss of control over parts of the business. If a disagreement arises with another firm in the network, the manager cannot fire the other firm's leaders. One firm cannot force another to do something; issues must be negotiated. Disagreements can lead to endless discussions. There is no tiebreaker to stop the discussions and initiate action. But a company can minimize these negatives by getting skillful at the partnering process, which will be described later in the chapter.

Designing the Virtual Corporation

The design of the organization, as usual, follows from the business strategy, but in this case the business strategy is the partnering strategy. What is unusual is that the partnering strategy is established independently of the organizational structure. Partnering is equally likely for functional, product, process, or market structures. The key organizational design issues that need to be addressed are the following:

- Partnering strategy
- External relationships
- Partner selection
- Partnership structure
- Supporting policies

Strategy is, of course, a crucial element—as it is in any organizational design. In the following discussion, though, the element that will need the most consideration is external relationships; this is the make-or-break issue in the virtual corporation's design.

Partnering Strategy

The business strategy of interest is the partnering strategy. Although the company's product and market strategy influences structure and internal lateral processes, as described in earlier chapters, the partnering strategy affects the lateral relationships between companies in the network. This strategy delineates the company's role in the network and determines the activities to own and perform and those to contract out. The organization design will coordinate and influence the contracted-out activities.

Company Role. A company can play different roles in a network, from specialist to network integrator for the entire business. A specialist performs one or a few activities and provides the service to everyone. A network integrator attempts to coordinate the activities performed by many firms, including itself, in order to create value for the ultimate customer.

Specialists attempt to become best in the world at the few activities they perform. Solectron and Flextronics manufacture printed circuit boards, for example. They manufacture more boards and invest more in process R&D than anyone else. Then they sell their services to network integrators in all industries in all countries. Why would any company want to manufacture printed circuit boards when it can buy them from Solectron? Federal Express does the same for distribution; Automatic Data Processing performs all payroll processing. Each is an expert and usually the lowest-cost provider in the specialty.

The network integrator is a firm that coordinates the decisions and actions of the companies making up the network. This firm takes the lead and manages the network as if it were a vertically integrated company. It formulates the strategy for the overall network, chooses member firms, and links them together with a telecom system. Nike, like Benetton, coordinates the work of independent factories in Asia and of retailers in all the markets that it serves. It coordinates all the work, from raw material to the customer, even though the work is performed by others.

A firm may choose to perform the entire integrating task, as Nike, Benetton, and Dell do, or it may integrate portions of the activities. If it integrates a portion of the total business, it may choose to link with peer firms that integrate complementary portions.

Thus the company's partnering strategy starts with the choice of role to play in the virtual corporation.

Activities of the Integrating Role. For companies taking on an integrating role, there is a choice among the activities to perform, own, and control and those to contract out. Usually, a company performs those activities that the customer finds important, those for which there are few outside suppliers, those that involve scale, those that integrate the members of the network, those that influence the brand, and those that give the firm an opportunity for competitive advantage. Commodities and input from plentiful or superior suppliers are contracted out.

A difficult choice must be made when an activity is important in the eyes of the customer, but outside suppliers are superior. The company can then invest to improve its own capability or form a close relationship with an outside supplier, hoping to manage its dependency and perhaps learn some of the needed skills.

Boeing is an example of a network integrator. Over the years it has managed the systems integration function and the difficult customer relationship, and, in terms of product, the cockpit—where all systems converge—and as much of the wings as it can retain. The rest is subcontracted to specialists around the world (which helps sell airplanes to airlines owned by governments). Boeing has thus strategically positioned itself to integrate the business, from raw material to customer, while performing about 20 percent of the actual work.

Boeing can also illustrate the dangers of contracting out. It recently contracted out the cockpit to Honeywell when it was overloaded with work. Honeywell developed some technology to complement its navigational systems. It seems to have achieved an

"Intel Inside" brand recognition that attracts customers and increases Honeywell's leverage on Boeing. Now Airbus is wooing the Japanese airframe manufacturers that have been part of Boeing's "team" of suppliers. To keep them—and the Japan Airlines orders—Boeing is offering them the wings on its next jumbo jet. Boeing will be challenged to maintain its control over the next airplanes and its status as the integrator.

Amazon.com yields yet another variation on the choice of what the integrator does and owns and what it contracts out. As suggested by the Boeing example, the make-or-buy decision is a continuous one. Amazon.com started as a "weightless" retailer. That is, it required minimal fixed assets. It contracted out the supplying of books to the largest book wholesaler. However, it discovered that wholesalers are good at sending truckloads to retailers. They are not good at sending a book or two to a consumer. So Amazon.com started inventorying the fastest-moving books and sending them from a company-owned warehouse. When Amazon.com added CDs and videos, it was even harder to find a wholesaler who could package two books, three CDs, and a video and send the package to a consumer address. Amazon.com knew how. But it was reluctant to teach a supplier. This supplier would make Amazon.com's knowledge available to Amazon.com's competitors. So Amazon.com built its own warehouses and took on the fulfillment function itself. It has been criticized for doing so. But, from Amazon.com's point of view, the step internalized a source of competitive advantage and made the company a fulfillment innovator. However, once other distributors like FedEx or UPS acquire the capability to fulfill small orders, it is probable that Amazon.com will sell its warehouses and buy the service from the low-cost provider.

Another example is Amazon.com's experience with toys. It added a number of new product lines to its repertoire in 1999. Amazon.com's early success with books was in providing the "World's largest selection" of books. Brick-and-mortar stores could not offer this choice nor carry the inventory. However, toys require a merchandising expertise. At Christmas it is less important to offer an infinite choice of toys than it is to have the right toy. It is important to have Cabbage Patch dolls and Furbies when people want them—and to have the buying clout to get more than your fair share from the toy manufacturers. So Amazon.com has married its e-commerce skill with the merchandising skill of Toys "R" Us. More joint ventures like this one are probably in Amazon.com's future. The pursuit of competitive advantage will lead companies to own an activity when there is an advantage and to outsource it when there is no advantage.

External Relationships

Once a company has chosen its role in the network and decided which activities to perform and which to contract out, it needs to design processes to coordinate the activities performed by others. Communication and joint decision processes are needed to manage the interdependence between the companies in the network. These external relationships are similar in many ways to the internal lateral processes of a firm and the types, and amounts of coordination among them similarly vary. Thus the task of the organizational designer is once again to match the types and amounts of coordination with the appropriate types and amounts of external lateral relationships.

The design choice is governed by the type of external relationships. These vary from a market relationship between buyer and seller to contracts between parties to sourcing and alliance arrangements to equity relationships to outright ownership. The continuum is shown in Figure 9.1, where the relationships are linked with the amount of coordination required and the amount of dependence on the outside firm. The relationships at the top are the cheapest and easiest to use. As the designer proceeds down the list, the relationships become more complex and require more management time and effort. The designer should proceed only until the point of coordination required by the partnering strategy is reached.

Another factor that influences the type of relationship between

Relationships	Relative strength	Coordination	Dependence	Value capture
	Strong			High
Ownership		Great deal	Very high	
Equity		Great deal	High	
Sourcing and alliance		Substantial	Moderate	
Contract		Occasional or some	Minimum	
Market		None	Zero	
	Weak			Low

FIGURE 9.1. Types of External Relationships and Coordination Requirements.

partners is value capture. For example, when Microsoft forms a relationship with a software partner, it often takes a minority equity stake. The stock will probably rise on the announcement of the partnership, so Microsoft takes an equity stake to capture some of that value. A different situation arises with biotechnology firms like Monsanto and Syngenta. They discover genes that can be inserted into seeds like corn or soy beans to help the plants resist pests and thus decrease the need for insecticides. But it's impossible to sell genes alone. The genes must be embedded in seeds that are sold to farmers. The value of the biotech firms' research can be captured only through the sale of the seeds, which motivated the biotech companies to take equity stakes in the seed companies. These stakes became joint ventures and then acquisitions. The acquisitions helped speed new genes to market, capture value for the biotech firm, and deny access to the seed company by other biotech firms.

Markets and Contracts. Markets and contracts are standard mechanisms for mediating economic transactions. Figure 9.1 shows that relationships mediated by markets require little coordination and communication between the parties. Indeed, the purchase of commodities from spot markets takes place between buyers and sellers who remain unknown to each other. Markets are used to secure products and services that are standard and freely available.

The contract relationship is somewhat more involved. The buyer and seller communicate and negotiate terms periodically, but there is little subsequent contact unless exceptions arise. Contracts come to pass when the items being acquired are not standard and are not always available. Some items may need to be customized, others may be standard but subject to shortages—like dynamic random access memory chips (DRAMs) for personal computers. A contract guarantees the source of supply for the length of the contract and specifies the customization.

Sourcing and Alliances. Sourcing and alliance relationships require more coordination. Sourcing involves a contract, but it involves a closer and longer-term relationship than the spot contracts discussed in the preceding paragraph. Usually the parties reveal their long-term plans to one another and participate in jointly developing products and services. For example, automobile companies are becoming more like network integrators and forming sourcing relationships with suppliers. Ford may choose TRW to supply all passenger safety equipment—seat belts, air bags, and so on. TRW then has to share its technology and development plans as part of its side of the bargain. Ford shares its car development plans with TRW, which may design safety equipment unique to Ford. TRW may have to invest in special equipment to make the unique products. Ford may then make TRW the sole supplier of the total volume to justify TRW's investment.

This kind of sourcing relationship has several characteristics. One is the substantial customizing by the supplier for the unique advantage of the customer. In return, the customer makes the customizer the sole or preferred supplier, as in the Ford/TRW example, which reduces the risk for the supplier and ensures the volume to pay for the effort. Sourcing relationships also involve a great deal of communication about future plans and coordination of product and service development. The parties become partners, jointly developing the unique product. There is usually a formal product development team with representatives from both parties. As with internal lateral processes, there will be an integrator (a product manager from the vendor), so that the product development team can span both companies. The partners will share the same computer-aided design system and design information. After the product is designed, the ordering and supplying will be done electronically as well. Thus, sourcing relationships are fewer, closer, longer-term relationships.

Although the terminology is not standard, similar relationships between competitors (as opposed to between suppliers and customers) are usually referred to as alliances (or *teaming,* in aerospace). The parties in an alliance also exchange information and commitments and jointly perform an activity and share the outcome. For example, IBM and Siemens formed an alliance to jointly develop the process technology for manufacturing the next generation of DRAMs. Each subsequently produced and marketed the product independently. Motorola and Toshiba formed an alliance to exchange technologies. Toshiba provided manufacturing process technology for DRAMs; Motorola provided microprocessor technology. The technologies were transferred during joint development of products using the technologies.

In each case, development teams are staffed by both partners. There is an integrator role to coordinate the joint effort and manage the relationship. A great deal of coordination and communication between the partners is essential to the joint activity.

Equity Relationships. The equity relationship is so named because it involves the transfer of equity. There are three main types of arrangements for the transfer of equity. In some cases the network integrator takes a minority shareholding in a supplier. Ford, for example, invested in Cummins Engine for a 20 percent stake and in Mazda for a 25 percent stake. The amounts vary, but the network integrator takes a substantial—although minority—position. In other types of equity relationships, each member takes a small stake in the others. Although they are unwinding at present, these cross-shareholdings were typical in Japan and some European countries. These cross-share holdings are used in alliances among equals. The most involved equity relationship is the joint venture. Here, a separate company is created with its own equity, which is usually split more or less equally between the parties.

Thus equity relationships can be joint ventures, cross-share holdings, or minority stakes, each with varying amounts of equity involved. They are alliances with a lot of control and a significant investment. There may be as much need for coordination and communication as in an alliance, but one or both partners may be more dependent and vulnerable. The exchange of equity symbolizes both greater commitment and longer-term commitment. An equity relationship is usually more difficult to unwind than an alliance, which may even have a termination date.

Equity relationships are used when the dependency cannot be covered by normal contractual terms and conditions. In the example of Ford and TRW, an equity relationship may not be necessary. TRW is vulnerable in this relationship because Ford may reveal TRW's technology to another supplier and demand a lower-cost proposal from that supplier. Ford is vulnerable because TRW could slightly modify the Ford product and sell it to General Motors or Honda. The parties could, however, agree to nondisclosure clauses and noncompetitive products for a two-year period. At the end of two years, all competitors will have reverse-engineered the product and discovered the technology, anyway. So if each partner adheres to the contractual agreement, the vulnerabilities of all are protected.

Enduring advantages, those that are critical or cannot easily be copied, usually need more protection. In certain cases, one partner may have an enormous incentive to use the proprietary information. In circumstances such as these, an equity exchange aligns the partners' interests and gives them more control over the relationship. The equity is intended to be a long-term bond of trust.

Ownership. Equity is not a guarantee that the partnership will not fall apart. It increases the probability of success at a cost. The ultimate control is 100 percent ownership of an activity. If the vulnerability is too great for one partner, or the opportunity for profit too large to share, one of the partners will purchase the other.

The application software unit of Apple is a good example. When the Mac first appeared, little application software was available for it. So Apple started its own software unit, which created MacPaint and MacDraw. Outside software houses became interested in creating software for the Mac, but they were reluctant to share information because Apple's in-house unit was a competitor. Apple decided to make the unit, called Claris, a separate company while maintaining a minority interest. But just before Apple's public stock offering, it pulled Claris back into the company. The reason? Microsoft had introduced Windows, and Claris was the software company with the most experience writing programs for Windows-type operating systems. With ten times as many Windows-compatible computers as Macs, an independent Claris would have a strong incentive to write primarily for Windows and secondarily for the Mac. But as a wholly owned unit of Apple, Claris would support the Mac first. Apple needed full control of Claris to keep that company's interests aligned with its own.

So three factors—coordination, vulnerability, and value capture—drive companies to choose more complex forms of relationship. Alliances and sourcing relationships are adopted to achieve the coordination needed to execute customization and joint development; markets and simple contracts are insufficient by themselves. But working jointly with other companies increases the vulnerability of the firm. Equity exchanges reduce the vulnerability and increase the firm's commitment and control and allow greater value capture. The combination of increased coordination, reduced vulnerability, and value capture drive organization designers to choose the more complex relationships.

Partner Selection

The choice of partner is crucial in alliances and equity relationships. (There is less dependence and vulnerability with market and contract relationships.) Firms that are skilled at alliances and equity ventures continuously and thoroughly evaluate potential partners.

The first priority when selecting a partner is to understand the potential partner's strategic intentions. Ford's intention may be to develop TRW as its safety equipment partner. Another auto manufacturer may use a partnership to learn TRW's technology and create its own internal capability. It may then use its internal capability to supply its own needs or to negotiate lower prices from TRW, having stripped it of its technical edge. Knowing these intentions in advance is the key to partner selection. Other factors include compatibility of goals, values, styles, time horizons, and so on.

Corning, a skilled partner, continuously locates partner candidates and assigns them to the company's officers. The top manager then investigates the candidate; a consulting firm analyzes the company and its history. Corning has found that it can learn more about a company's values by assessing its behavior in the face of adversity. It investigates what the company did during an event such as a plant closure, a hazardous waste spill, and so on. Corning then gets to know the candidate's managers, inviting them to speak at meetings or attend the annual officers meeting; it has them bring their spouses and gets to know them informally. A small joint project may be next. In this way, people at various working levels get to know one another. Each contact is a test. If a candidate passes all of them, Corning may try an alliance. If successful, it may try a larger alliance, evolve toward an equity relationship, and eventually suggest a joint venture. The selection process is continuous and thorough.

The selection process requires a lot of time and effort from management. However, this degree of up-front effort is characteristic of successful partnering. As the old saying goes, "You pay me now or you pay me later." Issues not discovered in the courtship will arise later in the partnership. They are more difficult to solve then, and the relationship more difficult to dissolve.

Today, the evaluation of partner candidates is getting easier. More companies now have a partnering history that can be exam-

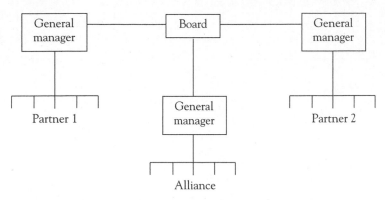

FIGURE 9.2. Partnership Structure for Sourcing, Alliances, or Joint Ventures.

ined. Indeed, in the future, being seen as an attractive partner will be a requirement for competitiveness. Thus the need to gain a good reputation as a partner actually controls certain temptations to behave opportunistically in alliances. More and more companies are investing in the up-front courtship process to find appropriate partners for longer-term relationships.

Partnership Structure

Alliances and joint ventures are joint activities that need to be structured. There are three types of structures for joint activities (Killing, 1983). In the *operator model* one partner takes the management responsibility for the joint activity. In the *shared model* responsibility is divided between the two partners. And finally, and primarily, in *joint ventures*, the joint activity can be autonomous.

The basic model for the partnership structure is shown in Figure 9.2. The two-partner structures shown in the figure may be any of those already discussed in Chapter Three. The alliance (or venture) itself is probably a functional structure focused on developing and supplying a product, service, or technology. Members from both partners form a board to supervise the activity.

The operator model is used in sourcing arrangements and sometimes in alliances and joint ventures. In the Ford/TRW example,

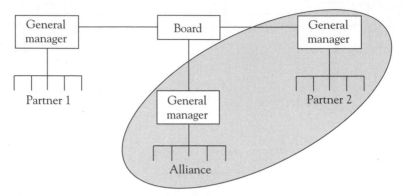

FIGURE 9.3. The Operator Alliance Model.

TRW probably serves as the operator and manages the product development effort. Ford contributes some people to work on the product and several managers to serve on the board. But the alliance manager and key functional managers are from TRW. The decision-making orientation is illustrated by the shading in Figure 9.3. The board acts much like a normal board of directors, reviewing work, approving investments, and agreeing on the selection of key people.

In the General Motors/Toyota joint venture, Toyota was the operator. Toyota wanted to learn how to manage in the United States and how to partner with the United Auto Workers. General Motors wanted to learn Toyota's production system. Both objectives were served by having Toyota manage the joint venture even though ownership was fifty-fifty.

The Motorola/Toshiba relationship involves an exchange of operator roles. Toshiba was the operator on the DRAM alliance, where it was the expert. Motorola was the operator on the micro-processor alliance, where it was the expert.

The operator model has been more successful than the shared model. It makes one company responsible. It minimizes conflicts. It leads to faster decisions. This model is preferred when one partner has the capabilities to manage the efforts and also works best when the role can be rotated between partners, as in the Motorola/Toshiba example.

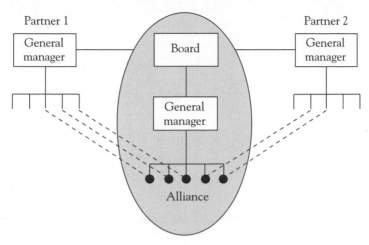

FIGURE 9.4. The Shared Alliance Model.

The shared model, used in many alliances and joint ventures, is preferred when each partner brings a complementary skill. Before the acquisition of Mazda, when Ford and Mazda formed an alliance to create a new car, they shared the responsibility. For small cars, Mazda provided the product development, engineering design, and manufacturing skills, while Ford provided the styling, finance, and marketing competencies. They divided the work based on skills and shared overall management responsibility. The focal point of decision-making shifts with this relationship, as illustrated in Figure 9.4.

The shared model is characterized by a small and active board. Usually, the board consists of four or five—no more than seven—people. It is staffed with two managers from each partner and the alliance general manager. This general manager comes from one partner and one of the managers from the other partner chairs the board.

A difficulty of the shared model is the potential for conflict among the partners or indecision. Indecision is likely if managers in the partner organizations interfere instead of using the board as the decision-making focal point. But if the partners are skilled at alliances and joint ventures and if the board is active, the partnership can capitalize on the combination of the complementary skills.

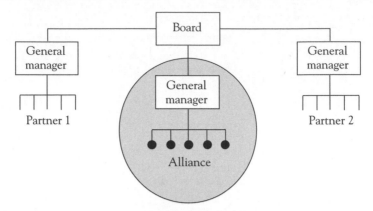

FIGURE 9.5. The Autonomous Joint Venture Model.

The third type of structure is the autonomous model, shown in Figure 9.5. In this model, the decisions are made by the venture itself, which becomes more independent of its parents. Usually the autonomous model is adopted by joint ventures. A venture usually begins by using the operator or shared model and evolves into the autonomous model. As the venture becomes successful and grows its own talent, it becomes less dependent on its parents. The board becomes an ordinary board; the major decisions are made within the venture. The benefit is that the venture can then act more quickly to deal with changing business situations.

Supporting Policies

The design of the virtual corporation is completed with the creation of supporting policies corresponding to the two remaining elements of the star model: the selection and development of people and the reward system. Both are enlisted to create behaviors, values, and norms that support the partnering process.

Many of the same skills that facilitate lateral internal processes also facilitate processes between companies. Particularly key are an ability to influence without authority and a facility for working with people from different cultures. Often, people can graduate from participation in internal processes to external ones.

The other people issue is the selection and development of people who can deal with the dilemma of partnering. That is, they must reveal information and cooperate with partners but must not reveal certain critical pieces of information. Part of this people issue is choosing individuals who can walk this fine line and be comfortable. The other part is training them to understand the aspects of the company's strategy and core competencies that should not be revealed. As more and more people work in direct contact with people from other companies, this training will become crucial.

The reward system needs to be augmented to encourage employees to look for the win-win outcome. Managers at Corning all tell stories of bosses who have reprimanded them for not looking for a benefit for the other partner. Partnering has to be good for both parties. Effective companies promote the seeing of the situation through the partners' eyes.

For example, one company is reevaluating its partnering approach. It has always tried to win in negotiations. And last year it won a very nice royalty agreement from its Japanese partner. But this year, it is not celebrating: the royalty is so favorable that the partner has no incentive to fulfill the partnership. The company is currently renegotiating so that both partners can profit from the relationship. Thus the reward system needs to promote a constant search for the win-win outcome.

The virtual corporation is a new name for groups of companies that contract out to one another. The network of companies that is formed acts collectively as if it were an integrated company.

In a virtual corporation, the key choices for the individual firm are its role in the network and the specific activities it will perform, own, and control. The organization design choices are the type of relationships among firms, the firms to work with, the structure of the joint efforts, and the development of employees to participate in partnerships.

10

Organizing the Continuous Design Process

The organization design tools described in these chapters can make a substantive difference in the efficient operation of a company. But taking information from page to boardroom can be an arduous journey. This chapter describes issues to be on the lookout for and methods to help manage some of the stresses that always seem to accompany change.

The Organization Design Process

Organization design is a process; it is a continuous process, not a single event. To keep the process continuous and current, a sequence for changing design policies is required. But the right mind-set in managers is also required.

Leaders must learn to think of *organize* as a verb, an active verb. Organizing is a continuous management task, like budgeting, scheduling, or communicating. Too often, organization is seen as synonymous with structure, which changes infrequently. In today's world, a good organization is one that lasts long enough to get you to the next one. A continuously changing business environment requires a continuously changeable organization to keep pace.

The time line shown in Figure 10.1 illustrates how today's company evolves toward the future organization. Not surprisingly, the future organization is guided by the future strategy, with the addi-

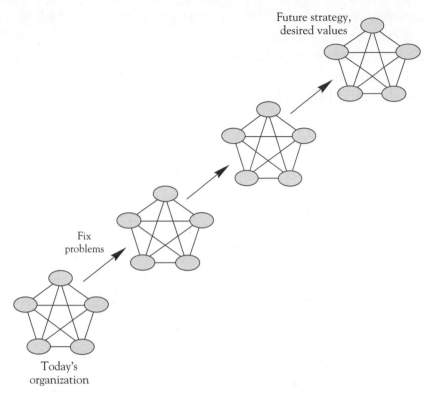

Future strategy,
desired values

Fix
problems

Today's
organization

FIGURE 10.1. Continuous Organization Design.

tion of desirable values and attributes along the way. The future
strategy applies to the company two, three, or five years down the
road, depending on the predictability of the business environment.
This long-range strategy provides the criteria for choosing the
future organizational type, along with the values that the company
believes to be desirable. For example, some companies want to
become the employer of choice for certain segments of the population. These values also become criteria for evaluating alternative
design choices. The different priorities assigned to the various criteria also help determine the design choice.

At the other end of the time line is today's organization. It
should be assessed or diagnosed by how well it fits its current business environment. Management needs to make design changes to

fix what is not working today, but in a manner consistent with the organization of the future.

Other intervening design steps can also be placed on the time line. Information systems always seem to set the pace of change—and they tend to have long development times. With this exception, the trend today is toward accelerated change, high-velocity change. Still, developing new systems and training people can take longer than anticipated.

Design Sequence

As managers look at the star model they often ask, "Where do I start?" My preference is indicated by the layout of the star's components: begin with strategy and move clockwise, returning to some policies as you get smarter about the behavior needed to implement the strategy. The preferred sequence of design steps is shown in a more detailed manner in Figure 10.2.

As noted, strategy is the place to begin. The strategy sets the basic direction and generates the criteria for choosing the other policies. Next, the departmental structure that best executes the strategy should be designed. The department type (based on geography, functions, products) communicates priority in addressing the strategy. It forms the vertical structure across which the key processes will take place. If the structure is functional, the processes may be designed to be cross-functional new product teams or cross-functional work flow process teams.

For vertical structures and lateral processes to mesh effectively, the roles and responsibilities of functional managers and process teams need to be defined and clarified. Who is responsible for pricing, forecasting, or personnel assignments? Key people can then be selected for the various roles. Mismatches can lead to a redefinition of the roles and responsibilities.

Once chosen, these people will need the relevant information. Information systems design follows. The appropriate performance measures can now be deduced and rewards designed to motivate

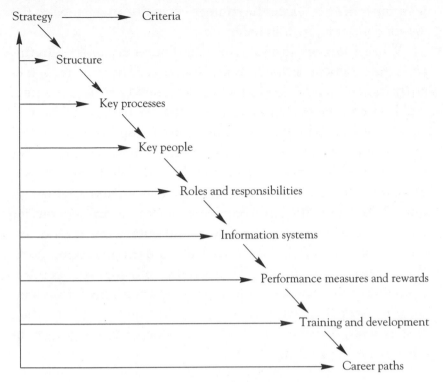

FIGURE 10.2. The Preferred Design Process.

appropriate behavior. Then the people can be trained and developed for their new roles in the organization. Finally, the designers can think their way through the career paths, so as to grow the talent needed for the various roles in the structure.

Although this process has a logical flow, it can encounter practical problems. What if the strategy is not clear? Without a clear strategy, the structure should not be changed. In turbulent industries, such as the multimedia industry today, the future is unknowable. Under such circumstances the designer should use the current structure or adopt a generic functional one and focus on processes. Processes are like organizational software; they are flexible and easily changed. So the designer should create some processes (teams, task forces) that manage the current business, lead to learning about the evolving new business, and allow the formulation of strategy as learning proceeds. Once the strategy crystallizes, a change to the appropriate structure is in order.

What if strategy always changes and never crystallizes? In this case, the designer continuously uses processes. The structure serves as the homeroom as people move from team to team. Reconfigurable project teams are the essence of the flexible organization.

Under some circumstances, different areas of the star model may seem to provide better starting points than strategy does. For example, people in the company may be complaining about compensation. In this case, the design process should begin with rewards because they will provide momentum and energy for change. However, to design a new reward system, one must determine what kind of behavior is needed—and this question invariably leads back to strategy. Thus strategy provides the focus no matter where the starting point is. Actually where one starts is arbitrary; it is more important to touch all policy areas on the star than to start at any particular place. The star model and strategy eventually provide the guidance.

How Do I Choose the Right Structure?

The plan for changing the organization emerges by plotting the sequence of changes on a time line. As noted, the first changes should work to fix current problems and, through a sequence of steps, evolve in a continuous fashion to the future organization. The choice of structures and processes is made essentially by assigning a priority to the possible dimensions of the organization—functions, geography, products, markets, and processes. The priority comes from the strategy—and particularly from the diversity of the business.

The decision process, therefore, begins with an analysis of the diversity of the business, as illustrated in Figure 10.3. The first cut at structure is determined by whether the business is service- or product-based, and whether it produces a single line of products and services or multiple lines. This framework contains four possible

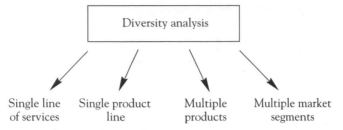

FIGURE 10.3. The First Step in Choosing a Structure.

basic starting points, because a business may consist of a single line of services, a single line of products, multiple product lines, or multiple market segments.

Let us start with examples of service businesses that offer a single line of services—an advertising agency and a group of pizza restaurants. The decision process for such companies is shown schematically in Figure 10.4. Following the diversity analysis model, the next question for a service business is whether it serves multiple and distinct geographical areas. If the advertising agency serves a single region, it will probably adopt a functional structure, the typical structure for a single-line business. For the ad agency, the functional structure would be one in which specialists such as writers, artists, TV programmers, and so on would form departments. Account executives in another department would manage the customer relationship. The remaining functions would be administrative departments such as human resources and finance.

The organization designer then moves to the next priority in the decision process. For the ad agency, the customers would come next. An agency's work is to put together advertising programs for existing customers or to propose campaigns for new ones. These programs would be developed by formal cross-specialty teams. Because the requirements of a customer program are constantly changing, the agency would not want to hardwire the cross-specialty or customer teams into the organization. The account executive would coordinate the team and provide the link to the customer. Thus the organization for an agency would consist of

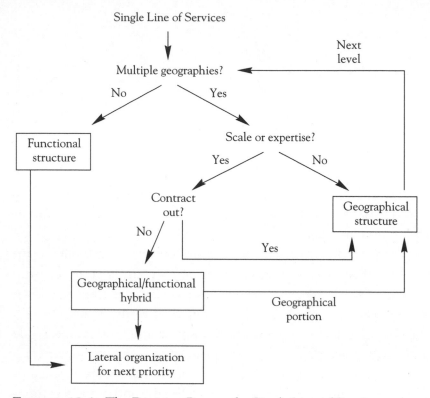

FIGURE 10.4. The Decision Process for Single Line of Service Businesses.

specialist groups (functions) that serve as homerooms for the development of specialists, functional experts, and specialty tools. However, the actual work of developing a customer program or targeting an advertising campaign would be performed by cross-specialty teams.

The third priority would be processes for managing money and people. The finance and human resources departments act as integrators and design the processes for managing these phenomena. They work informally with key people in each department and with formal cross-departmental teams when changing the design of budgeting or recruiting processes.

In this manner, the designer moves through the decision process by considering all the different organizational dimensions and assign-

FIGURE 10.5. Geographical Structure.

ing priorities to them based on the strategy. In the case of a business providing a single service in a single geography, the structure is functional, with customer programs and administration processes the key management processes to be designed. The answer to the multiple geographies question in Figure 10.4 would have been yes.

For the pizza chain, the geographies could represent different markets—urban or rural areas, or different ethnic groups within the geographies. There may also be different local competitors. Thus each distinct geographical area could become a profit center.

The remaining issue is whether any activities require scale or expertise. That is, are any activities needed to deliver the service that cannot achieve minimum efficient scale within the geographical area? If the answer is yes, then another question must be asked. Can the scale or expertise be contracted out?

Let us use the pizza chain as an example. The purchasing function may provide an opportunity for buying supplies for all restaurants in all geographies. However, if all suppliers are local or there is little buying leverage, there is no scale effect. The structure chosen in this case would be the geographical one illustrated in Figure 10.5. Each region becomes a single geography providing a single line of services. The next structure decision shifts to the level below the geographies. The flow chart in Figure 10.4 shows that the decision process returns to the functional organization below each geography and the previous analysis is repeated.

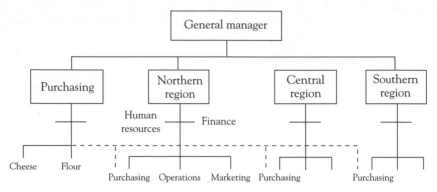

FIGURE 10.6. Hybrid Functional/Geographical Structure.

However, there may be some vendors who can supply all regions. By concentrating purchases with these vendors, significant savings in food costs may be achieved. If buying is a key skill not to be contracted out, the purchasing function probably will be centralized. The resulting structure would be a functional/geographical hybrid like the one shown in Figure 10.6. As with all hybrids, linkage between the two dimensions is critical. In this example, cheese and flour are purchased centrally and other ingredients are purchased locally. Cross-geography linkage is provided by the central purchasing function, which chairs a team of local purchasing people from each region.

After the purchasing, or scale function, is broken out and organized centrally, the remaining activities—operations, marketing, and so on—are organized into three regions as before. Also as before, each region is organized functionally.

Another possibility illustrated by Figure 10.4 is that of the need for expertise, such as real estate expertise. The choice and purchase of sites for new stores, as well as the sale of redundant sites, requires specific real estate knowledge. Rather than have each regional manager (who is not an expert in real estate), choose and buy or lease sites, a central activity like purchasing could be created. Or the activity could be contracted out to local professionals. When contracting out for scale or expertise, the decision process returns to a regional structure, as shown in Figure 10.5.

Thus a business offering a single line of services could result in a functional structure, a geographical structure, or a functional/ geographical hybrid. The key strategic issues are whether the service is delivered across multiple distinct geographies and whether any of the activities require scale or expertise beyond what can be provided in a single geography. The functional structure is complemented by a lateral organization focused on customer programs and projects. The geographical structures are usually complemented by lateral coordination processes for functions and products or services. The type and amount of lateral processes vary with the function and amount of new product or service development.

The purchasing function described earlier yielded buying leverage for some commodities and was centralized for them (Figure 10.6). The central function then played the integrator role and chaired the cross-geographical purchasing team for coordinating other policies and practices. An operations integrator can be used to chair an operations team when there are frequent changes in operating technologies and practices. A team can share best practices without an integrator if operation technologies are not very dynamic. There may also be a marketing integrator if there is a common brand shared across the geographies. The central marketing group will manage the brand along with cross-geographical advertising and promotion. A cross-geographical marketing team would coordinate best practices and manage promotions that cross several regions. Human resources and finance would be treated similarly. Figure 10.7 shows the lateral processes added to the hybrid structure introduced in Figure 10.6.

If the restaurant pursues a strategy of competing by offering new menu items, it will need to design a new product development process that crosses functions and geographies. It may need a small R&D unit staffed with food science experts. It probably will need product managers in marketing, who will manage the new product development process. Initially, products would be developed by teams consisting of R&D, operations, purchasing, and product management from marketing. These teams would work out of the

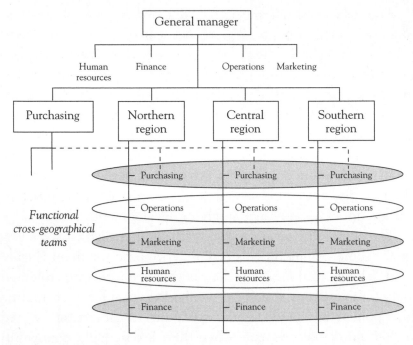

FIGURE 10.7. Hybrid Functional/Geographical Structure with Functional Integrators and Teams.

corporate headquarters, as shown in Figure 10.8. The products would be rolled out to the regions and the responsibility transferred to cross-functional teams within each region. When a product is launched and becomes a standard menu item, the sponsoring team would disband or prepare for the next new item. In this manner, the single line of service business develops capabilities for executing strategies requiring a geographical, functional, and new product or service focus.

The possible structures for single product line businesses are shown in Figure 10.9. Single product line businesses have traditionally been functionally structured. Today, the key questions are whether the business competes on speed and requires fast cycles. If speed is required, the best structure is one based on work flow processes, such as order fulfillment, new product development, and so on. Here functions would get second priority but would be coor-

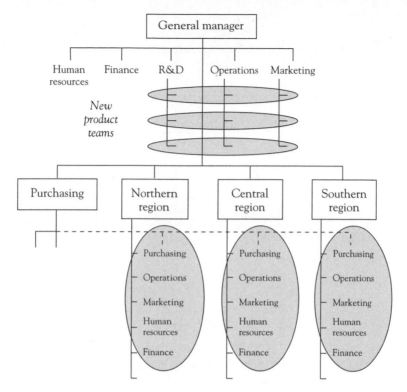

FIGURE 10.8. Hybrid Structure Plus Product Teams.

dinated with lateral management processes. If long cycles are acceptable, the best structure would be primarily functional with lateral work flow process coordination.

It is also possible for a service business to require a geographical structure. If the product has a low value-to-transport cost ratio and low minimum efficient scale levels, it is possible to create geographical profit centers, as shown in Figure 10.5. Cement and cardboard packaging are examples of such service businesses. The analysis for the service business can also apply to the single-product business and will not be repeated here.

The diversity analysis might conclude that the business is a multiproduct one, like Gillette, which makes razors and blades, personal care products, pens, and small electric products such as Braun razors. Similarly it could conclude that the business is a multiservice

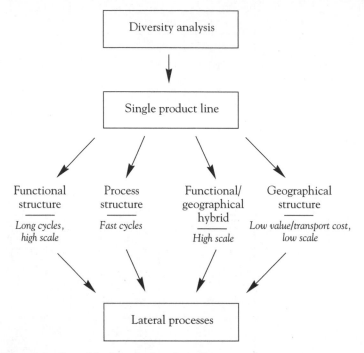

FIGURE 10.9. Possible Single-Product Business Structures.

one, like Merrill-Lynch, which provides investment banking, bro-kerage, and trading services. Or it may indicate a multimarket busi-ness like Citibank, which engages in consumer banking, commercial banking, and other services for individuals with high net worth. The decision process for these types of organizations is shown in Figure 10.10. The typical outcome is a multibusiness, multiple-profit-center structure based on different things: product lines for Gillette, markets for Citibank, and service lines for Mer-rill-Lynch. Each profit center is itself a single line of business.

At this point, the analysis for single-line businesses can be applied to each profit center. They may be organized by function, process, or geography and the other dimensions will be prioritized and organized laterally.

The other possibilities are the hybrids, either functional or front/back. The functional product hybrid was shown and discussed

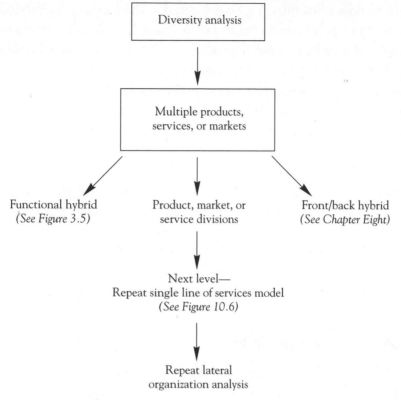

FIGURE 10.10. Decision Process for Structure and Processes of Multiple Businesses.

in Chapter Three. The functional geographical hybrid was discussed earlier in this chapter and is shown in Figure 10.6. The front/back model for products, markets, and geographies was discussed in Chapter Eight. After the basic structure is chosen, the front and back portions are analyzed to determine if they should be functional, process, or geographic. The lower-priority dimensions become the basis for the lateral organization.

Thus the process begins with a diversity analysis, which helps the decision maker choose the basic type of structure. Once the multiple profit center model has been defined, whether it is products or services, markets or geographies, or hybrids, a second analysis determines the structure within each division. For example, a multiproduct business may be organized at the top level by product units, but each product unit may be organized functionally, geographically, or by process, depending on the analysis derived within each product division. The analysis continues to examine all dimensions and to specify types and amounts of lateral coordination. For example, for the single-line pizza restaurant that operated in different, distinct geographies, the structure was regional divisions. Each region was further structured into functions. Lateral coordination across regions for each function took place through teams and integrators. New product development teams were the third dimension of the pizza restaurant business structure when it decided to compete by offering new menu items.

The completion of the design process should lead to a choice of structure and of lateral processes. The next step is to define the roles of the managers in the new organization more clearly.

Roles and Responsibilities

The process of defining roles and responsibilities begins after the structure and lateral processes have been designed. After any change to the organization, each employee will want to know "What is my role?" Whether working with lateral processes inside the company or executing alliances across partner companies, the question is always "Who is responsible for what?" One of the most useful tools in implementing any organization design is the responsibility chart, shown in Exhibit 10.1.

The structure defines which roles need definition. It is best to stick to only two levels of structure for this exercise. As shown in the chart, the roles form the (vertical) columns. The key decisions that these roles will execute form the (horizontal) rows. These decisions are likely to be contentious. They are the ones around which the turf and territory issues are likely to surface.

To create the chart, the people who play the roles listed in the columns are interviewed. They suggest which decisions should be listed. It is best to list about thirty-five decisions. Too few decisions

EXHIBIT 10.1. Responsibility Chart for a Financial Services Organization.

Decisions \ Roles	Sales	Segment marketing	Insurance	Mutual funds	Marketing council	CEO	Finance	Human resources	Regional team
Product price									
Package design									
Package price									
Forecast	A	R	C	C	C	I	I	X	X
Product design									

Note: For clarity, only one line of the matrix has been completed.

will not provide the clarity needed to know who is responsible for what. Too many will require a laborious effort to define the roles; it will seem too bureaucratic.

After the matrix is completed, the people playing the roles fill out the matrix individually. They answer the question, "How should we make decisions in the new organization?" To complete the matrix, they need a language to describe the different ways that a role can affect a decision. Four is the usual number, with no formal role a fifth option:

R = Responsible

A = Approve

C = Consult

I = Inform

X = No Formal Role

The person who is responsible for making a decision is given an R in the appropriate box. The segment marketing group, for example, is responsible for the forecast. That is, the segment marketing people initiate the process, collect the information, maintain the database for it, and arrive at a forecast.

Ideally, there would be one R for each row and no entries of any other kind. However, in multidimensional organizations, other types of roles are at play in joint decisions. For example, the sales function does not do the forecast but must approve it. That is, sales must concur with the forecast before segment marketing can implement it. Therefore, sales's box gets an A. If there is no agreement, segment marketing and sales must negotiate. Again, sales cannot overturn the forecast, but must agree with it. If there is still no agreement, the issue is raised to the CEO for resolution. Others may not be required to approve a decision, but they must be consulted by the responsible party. The C placed in the box for the general managers and the marketing council signifies that segment marketing must get input from them before making a commitment. However, once having gotten their input, segment marketing can decide what to do; it does not need their agreement. It only needs to consult with the parties who have been given Cs.

Finally, some roles do not need to be involved in a decision before it is made but do need to know the outcome afterward. For example, the finance function needs to know the forecast so that it can make cash forecasts and so on. But finance does not need to participate in the forecast itself. Finance needs to be informed, so it is given an I in the appropriate box. Others have no formal role in this decision. If those given an R want to involve them, that is fine. These people receive an X.

After each role occupant has completed the chart, everyone meets, usually off-site, for a half day or a full day to discuss and reach agreement on the role assignments. Usually, the results of the individual matrix assessment are displayed. There is almost always complete disagreement. The disparity motivates a lively discussion. A facilitator then proceeds, decision by decision. For each decision, the discussion revolves around why a person should participate. What value does that person provide? Is it worth the complexity and possible time delay? This discussion is the real value of the exer-

Strategic fit	**X**	Commitment to implement	**=**	Effectiveness

FIGURE 10.11. Design Effectiveness.

cise. People begin to talk about how they will work together. They teach one another about their roles. In the end, there is usually consensus and a completed matrix. If there is no consensus, then the CEO must say, "Okay, I have heard the arguments. Most people prefer this way. Let's try it and see if it works. We'll review the outcomes in three months. Next decision."

In either case, in the end the matrix is completed. To define a role, one simply proceeds down the column under the role title. The entries become the assignments. The process educates the participants and creates consensus about roles and responsibilities. The matrix provides the clarity needed in the flexible, ever-changing organizations of today. If another change is made to the organization, the chart is simply redrawn. It is a tool that can be used frequently and disseminated throughout the organization as needed.

Design Effectiveness and Implementation

How can the effectiveness of an organization design be gauged? There are two aspects to effectiveness, as shown in Figure 10.11.

Organization designs are effective when they achieve a strategic fit. A *strategic fit* occurs when all the policies in the star model are aligned with the strategy and reinforce one another. A strategic fit means effectiveness because congruence among the policies sends a clear and consistent signal to organization members and guides their behavior.

Also contributing to effectiveness is the amount of *commitment* among organization members to implement the design. Management needs to follow a design process that builds this commitment. Neither fit nor commitment is sufficient by itself; both are needed.

Most of this book has been devoted to the process of achieving a strategic fit. In this last section, I will briefly describe a process for building commitment to implement the design. This is a process that I have developed and used over the years. (For a more complete presentation of these implementation processes see Mohrman and Cummings, 1989.)

The Organization Design Process

The process discussed in this section is one of teaching people how to design their own organization. This organization design process, shown in Figure 10.12, begins with the general manager and the group reporting directly to the general manager, hereafter called the executive team. These are the people whose organization is to be designed. The process is presented to them and shaped by them to fit their circumstances. The purpose of the discussion is to get the executive team comfortable with an open design process.

Development of Criteria and Alternative Structures

The first step is a kickoff workshop, which lasts about three days. The first half day includes an educational presentation, during which the ideas in this book are presented and discussed. The purpose of the presentation is to give everyone a shared framework and language, as well as some ideas about current best practices. There is no limit to the size of the group that attends this first session. Usually everyone who will participate in the design effort is either present or connected by videoconference. Often the session is videotaped for viewing by those who are absent or any others who wish to see the presentation and discuss it with their work group. Books are provided when they are pertinent.

Much of the remaining time—usually at least two days—is devoted to the executive team or a subgroup of it, which becomes the design team. After a question-and-answer period covering the issues of the morning presentation, the design team reviews the

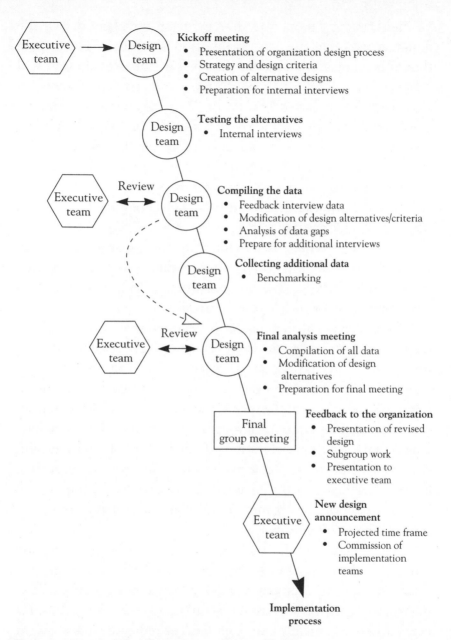

FIGURE 10.12. The Organization Design Process.

business strategy. From the strategy, team members derive the design criteria that the new organization is to satisfy. The criteria should be concrete statements about how the organization will behave: "We will deliver Product X no later than twenty-four hours after the customer has ordered it," or "We will generate a minimum of five viable new product ideas each month," or "We will improve quality by a factor of ten times each year." After coming up with about twenty-five criteria, the design team discusses them. It uses some procedure with which team members are familiar to choose and rank the criteria. The result should be about five key criteria, which will guide the design.

The strategy is then used to frame a future organization toward which the company will evolve. The alternatives to be designed are those that fix today's organizational problems and move the company toward tomorrow's desired organization.

The design team's next task is to create alternative designs using the process described earlier in this chapter. The alternative designs include structure and key lateral processes. Each alternative is discussed; the positives and negatives of each are listed. Depending on the size of the team and the number of alternatives, the design team can form subgroups or remain together to carry out this procedure. The design team then arrives at from one to three alternatives with which its members are comfortable. These alternatives must then be tested on the rest of the organization. The purpose of the test will be both to inform the organization of what the design team is considering and to solicit input.

The remainder of the workshop is taken up with planning and scheduling the interview process (for the test) among organization members. Part of this process is developing a standard interview format to define the presentation and questions to be asked. In some cases, when an organization is under cost-reduction pressure, for example, the organization design process is perceived as a head-count-reduction exercise. If this is the case, the design team members must be prepared to address those concerns during the interview process.

Testing the Alternatives

The design team members, either singly or in pairs, interview the sixty to seventy people who will be affected by any organizational change. Team members interview people in a part of the company for which they are not responsible. There are two reasons for this. First, team members learn about a new part of the company and, second, they tend to get more open responses to their questions. During the interview, the team member presents the design team's current thinking about the strategy, the criteria the team derived from the strategy, and the alternative organization structures (including any lateral processes) that it is proposing. The interviewees ask questions and critique the alternatives from their own vantage points. If they are not pleased with a particular alternative, they are asked to propose a countersolution. This is the interviewee's first opportunity to respond to the criteria or the alternative structures.

The interviews can take place in many ways. Ideally every organization member is interviewed individually, face to face. However, this is not always possible or practical. Key individuals should always receive individual attention, but others may be interviewed in groups or through videoconferencing. The design team makes the trade-offs between time, resources, and the people to include. Often outside consultants can provide help and additional resources for interviews.

Compiling the Data and Modifying the Design

After completing the interviews, the design team must consolidate and analyze the responses. The team should gain a good idea of where the organization stands at this point. Is there an emerging consensus for all or parts of the alternatives? The design team then makes modifications to the criteria and the structure alternatives or to the emerging, preferred alternative, based on the organization's input. At this point, the design team can review progress with the executive team or other higher authorities as necessary.

A decision is usually made at this point either to go directly to the final meeting or to conduct another round of data collection and analysis. If there is an emerging consensus and time is critical, a company is likely to go directly to a final meeting. However, there may be several sticking points that require further work. These issues become the agenda for the next phase of design.

Benchmarking and Collecting Additional Data

One effective tool is the benchmarking visit. Other companies that have wrestled with the controversial issues or have solved them can be visited. These visits are best conducted at the stage when the design team knows what it needs to know more about. The groups visiting other companies can include design team members and others who may benefit from the experience.

Other workshops may be used to address specific topics. Experts from inside and outside the company may be convened to solve problems around an issue. The design team itself may probe more deeply into the issues.

Compiling Data and Preparing for the Final Meeting

The design team convenes to review the results of the second-phase analysis and to revisit the criteria and design alternatives. Modifications are made based on what the team has learned. At this point, the team tries to agree on a particular organizational alternative. A review with the executive team is again in order. Modifications to the alternative are made again in preparation for a presentation at the final meeting.

Feedback to the Organization

The final meeting is usually a day and a half or two days long and includes the top three levels of the organization and other key contributors. Between fifty and eighty people are usually present. These are the people who will be most affected by any changes. These are also the people who were exposed to the initial presentation and interviewed about the proposed alternatives. The purpose of the session is to update them on the design progress and to get their input one more time before committing to a particular design alternative.

The design team presents its analysis of the strategy and of the organization, the knowledge it gained during the process, its design criteria, and the recommended organizational alternative. After questions and answers, the group is broken into subgroups. Each subgroup is a cross-section of the company. The subgroups are usually carefully designed to get a good balance of constituencies and personalities. A member of the design team is assigned to each group to answer questions. Facilitators can also be used.

The task of each subgroup is to critique the proposed alternative. Any group member who disagrees with a portion of the proposed design must propose an alternative that meets the design criteria and then convince the other subgroup members. This process forces the subgroups to live with the general manager's problem and to act responsibly in making counterproposals. In this manner, the organization's members learn the strategy and the logic of the proposed organization. Their opinion is sought, heard, and used to modify alternatives before a final announcement is made.

Each subgroup meets for a half to a full day to reach its recommendation. The recommendations are made to the executive team at the end of the final meeting. The executive team and the general manager make their decision at this time, or shortly thereafter, based on the input of the organization.

Variations on the Design

There are variations in the design of the subgroups at the final meeting. Usually all groups get the same mission—to recommend an alternative for the entire organization. Sometimes, if an organization spans very large regions, two final meetings can be held, one in each region with cross-population of people from all of them. For example, one company had a meeting in Europe with some North Americans attending and another meeting in the United States with some Europeans attending. In this case, the organizations for Europe and North America were to be different, so the meeting in Europe naturally focused more on the European organization. Also, the organization was too complex to analyze as a whole. So different subgroups were given different portions of the design to look at. For example, two subgroups included predominantly members from the back end, the manufacturing and engineering side of the organization. Their task was to concentrate on the proposed structure for this area. In this way, people with pertinent information can have more say in the changes that affect them directly.

Other Design Process Issues

Using this design process increases the probability that a strategic fit will be obtained and that the people whose cooperation is needed to implement the design are kept informed and supportive. Of course, some people will still be skeptical—but no process is 100 percent effective. Using this process produces a higher probability of success in building commitment than you're likely to get with more centralized processes.

There are always some standard questions. "What will keep the organization from coming to a stop while the design process is taking place?" is one. The answer is that the organization does not come to a stop, but people do invest energy in lobbying for their preferred outcomes. Any time a reorganization is contemplated, such lobbying discussions will take place. The described process tries to get the discussions out on the table rather than behind closed doors. It gives people a chance to object before a change is made. If their opinions are not sought and heard beforehand, they will express them afterward as "pocket vetoes" or through passive resistance. It comes back to the pay-now-or-pay-later expression—the time to design and implement a change is shorter when objections are sought and responded to before making the change. This process invests more up-front design time and in doing so reduces the amount of implementation time.

Like any management process, the design process improves with experience. The first time is the toughest. But with repeated use, it will grow easier and easier. Today's need for frequent and rapid change makes skill at the design process a competitive advantage.

Another issue that will affect the process is the organization's trust in management. A frequently asked question is, "How does the organization know that management has not already decided on an alternative? This process could be seen as just a charade." This question is a good one. Management must train itself not to decide prematurely and to listen to new information. By listening and modifying alternatives, management can show good faith and earn trust. Over time, the organization will see the process as an opportunity to learn and to influence change.

If management decides the outcome ahead of time and uses this process to sell its decision, it will have only the worst of both worlds. It will have invested valuable management time in the design process and still meet with resistance after the new organization structure is announced. The design process outlined here will not serve any management that the organization does not trust. However, for a management team that is trustworthy, the process is an opportunity to earn the trust and even the admiration of the organization members.

The design process provides a thorough method of collecting quality information for a good strategic fit. It provides ample opportunities for affected parties to influence the outcome. Finally, it helps to build commitment within the organization for the implementation of change. Both fit and commitment are required for an organization design to be effective.

Conclusion

The key point of this analysis of organization design is that companies should choose among alternative organizations based on how well they meet criteria derived from the company's own business strategy, rather than by how fashionable they are in the business press. Some companies in business situations characterized by extremes of variety, change, and speed may well find that the fashionable alternatives meet their criteria. But others may not. In each case, they should choose what is effective, not what is attractive.

Any of the current organizational models—the process organization, the distributed organization, the virtual corporation, and the front/back organization design—can be effective in the right circumstances and for the right company. For each model, there will be forces favoring—and hindering—its choice. The star model presented in these pages generates a checklist of factors to be considered when designing an organization that will be aligned with its own goals and supported by policies that fit its purposes.

In conclusion, I wish to emphasize once again the role of leader. I see the leader as a *decision shaper* rather than a *decision maker*. The decision-shaping role is achieved through the organization design. The star model provides the management-controlled policies that will influence the way others make decisions.

References

Chandler, A. *Strategy and Structures*. Cambridge, Mass.: MIT Press, 1962.

Cohen, S. G. "Teams and Teamworks: Future Directions." In J. R. Galbraith and E. E. Lawler (eds.), *The Future of Organizations*. San Francisco: Jossey-Bass, 1993.

D'Aveni, R. A. *Hypercompetition: Managing the Dynamics of Strategic Maneuvering*. New York: Free Press, 1994.

Dertouzes, M. L., Lester, R. K., and Solow, R. M. *Made in America: Regaining the Productive Edge*. Cambridge, Mass.: MIT Press, 1989.

Dyer, W. G. *Team Building: Issues and Alternatives*. Reading, Mass.: Addison-Wesley, 1988.

Galbraith, J. R. "Designing the Innovating Organization," *Organization Dynamics*, Winter 1982, pp. 5–25.

Galbraith, J. R. *Competing with Flexible Lateral Organizations*. (2nd ed.) Reading, Mass.: Addison-Wesley, 1994.

Galbraith, J. R. *Designing the Global Corporation*. San Francisco: Jossey-Bass, 2000.

Galbraith, J. R., Downey, D., and Kates, A. *Designing Dynamic Organizations*. New York: AMACOM, in press.

Hall, A. "How the Web Is Retooling Detroit." *Business Week*, November 27, 2000, p. 193.

Hout, T., and Bower, J. "Fast Cycle Capability for Competitive Power." *Harvard Business Review*, Nov.-Dec. 1998, pp. 10–118.

Killing, P. *Strategies for Joint Venture Success*. New York: Praeger, 1983.

Lawler, E. E. *High-Involvement Management*. San Francisco: Jossey-Bass, 1986.

Lawler, E. E. *Strategic Pay: Aligning Organization Strategies and Pay Systems*. San Francisco: Jossey-Bass, 1990.

Lawler, E. E. III. "From Job-Based to Competency-Based Organizations." *Journal of Organization Behavior*, 1994, *15*, 3–15.

Lawler, E. E. *From the Ground Up*. San Francisco: Jossey-Bass, 1996.

Ledford, G. E. "Designing Nimble Reward Systems," *Compensation and Benefits Review*, July-Aug., 1995.

Mohrman S. A., Galbraith, J. R., and Lawler, E. E. *Tomorrow's Organization: Crafting Winning Capabilities in a Dynamic World*. San Francisco: Jossey-Bass, 1998.

"R&D Scoreboard." *Business Week*, June 1992.

Smith, D., and Katzenbach, J. *The Wisdom of Teams*. Boston: Harvard Business School Press, 1992.

Index